You Can Change Your World!

– MR PHIL –

FASTPRINT PUBLISHING
PETERBOROUGH, ENGLAND

FastPrint

www.fast-print.net/store.php

You Can Change Your World

All characters are fictional. Any similarity to any action person is purely coincidental

ISBN 978-184426-965-5

First published 2011 by
FASTPRINT PUBLISHING
Peterborough, England.

An environmentally friendly book printed and bound in England by www.printondemand-worldwide.com

Mixed Sources
Product group from well-managed forests, and other controlled sources
www.fsc.org Cert no. TT-COC-002641
© 1996 Forest Stewardship Council
FSC

PEFC Certified
This product is from sustainably managed forests and controlled sources
www.pefc.org
PEFC
PEFC/16-33-415

This book is made entirely of chain-of-custody materials

This book is dedicated to two people:

My Father: Mr. I A Akintunde

Dad you always wanted to write a book. I saw you slaving over your old typewriter, tap, tap, tap with your one finger style. Dad you never did write that book, but now through me, you have.

R.I.P

We all love you. (Your Children)

★★★★

My Wife: Adetokunbo Akintunde

Through thick and thin, understanding and most of the time not understanding, you have not only stuck by me, you have paid a huge price to make this happen.

In you I did find a good thing. I Love you.

Why I wrote this book...

This book was written to address the onslaught of change and uncertainty that has gripped the world for the last three, maybe four decades.

As I write, we are going through a credit crunch! People are losing their jobs, the housing market has collapsed – negative equity and repossessions abound, first-time buyers have little hope of getting on the property ladder, petrol prices keep rising and rising, the average income in the UK and US is plummeting and plummeting as inflation continues to rise.

That is of course not all! University graduates are catapulted into a market that has seen graduates coming out for many years to find there are no jobs, no prospects, and for the few opportunities available, they are engaged in fierce competition the likes of which one would not believe unless one is unfortunate to be one of the poor lot trying to find a job in our world today.

There is a quiet desperation in the air!

A desperation no one talks about or want to talk about, we feel it, sense it, taste it, but yet no one talks about it.

For some people this desperation has turned to perplexity.

The question is:

"How does a man or woman make it in today's brave new world?"

The answer you will find will emerge from the pages of this book. Now that is a very bold claim, I can literally hear you think, I understand why you will think that, I would think that myself if I haven't invested over 17years of my life studying, investigating, collating, refining and teaching what works. If I haven't seen my life and other people's lives change as a result of the kind of information this book will reveal to you.

This book was written with you in mind, and who are you?

You maybe a teenager with your whole life ahead of you, this book will provide you with priceless insights about the road ahead, sort of like a Sat. Nav. (Satellite Navigation) and traffic updates all rolled into one contraption.

For you as a teenager this is a tremendous advantage, it'll save you years of trial and error, giving you an opportunity to learn from the mistakes of many ahead of you in this journey called life.

You may be middle aged; you have tried everything and then some. You are almost ready to throw in the towel and shrug your shoulders saying "maybe it wasn't meant to be for me." You have worked hard, made money, sometimes even made a lot of money but still you are not where you think you ought to be. This book I believe will be for you a breath of fresh air. The content within this book has been a source of renewed hope for many. I believe that hope is the picture of your preferred future. This book is designed not only to rejuvenate you but to develop a long term relationship with you on your journey in life; this way there is no fear of building high hopes only for them to be dashed again. All we require from you is a commitment to stay the course. Your decision to commit to your better future is the only thing we cannot provide for you, however once the commitment is there, the rest as they say is a done deal.

Lastly maybe you are past the middle age stage of your life, now you are in the twilight of your journey, this book has got even better news for you. Come on this journey with us and we will reveal to you the tremendous opportunities you now have because of your experience.

This book is written to give you an edge, an advantage and the help we all need to get ahead and not miss our desired destination.

I boldly declare to you that without reservation that;

You can change your world!

Mr Phil's YOU Can CHANGE Your WORLD

Common Strategies for an Uncommon Life

Contents

The beginning of the belief that everyone can change their reality

Introduction

"People say you can't change the world! Yes, but you can change your world; and that's all the world you need changing anyhow." - Mr. Phil.

I have been privileged to experience first hand the power of changing my world. I am a British born Nigerian, who grew up in Nigeria and came back to reside in the UK at the age of 19. In my first week, to my surprise, I found myself straight on to the dole. Shortly after that I was adorned with my very own Burger King uniform and cap, where flipping burgers was my specialty, and after that secured an early morning and evening cleaning job, then went through a myriad of unskilled jobs, you think of it and I have probably done it... from all that to who I am today required me to drastically change my world.

Here is what you will get out of this book.

I will share with you some timeless principles in a practical way, i.e. through my personal experiences.

Through true life stories and personal experiences I will reveal what works. I will steer clear of aspects that I have not experienced or are not yet in my reality. Frankly, I am still a work in progress; I will not indulge in reaching for ideas or concepts that are currently not in my present reality.

Why?

It's important for me to keep this information authentic. I heard somewhere before; "To know and not to do, is not to know" in other words if one says they know, the proof that they really know is in their doing what they say they know. I grew up in Nigeria so I know what devastating results can be derived from, people thinking "they know", yet their actions show they don't have a clue! It is time to stop deluding ourselves.

"If you want to enjoy the rewards in reality, you can't afford to indulge in fantasy!" Mr. Phil.

Pause! Think about that!

This book is about what works, what has worked in the past, what works now and what will work in the future, and as long as time ticks they will continue to work. Principles are permanent while methods are temporal.

The truths that I share in this book are of such importance for a successful reality, that I often wonder why we don't hear them shouted off the roof tops! I appreciate I cannot assume everyone will be interested, but for those who are; it is surely nice to know where the advantages lie and where the pitfalls lurk.

Today my greatest passion is helping people change their world for the better. The truth is that anybody at anytime can change their world NOW! It doesn't involve acquiring a huge amount of education, or belonging to a certain class or attaining a certain status to be all we want to be - all it takes is desire!

The bigger the desire the quicker the change!

So, are you ready to change your world? If you are, let's go on a journey together.

Life is a Journey, success is a journey, changing your world is a journey.

Let's get started.

Mr. Phil.

Chapter 1

Why?

"Today Is the First Day of the Rest of Your Life"
Author Unknown

To change your world the first thing you need to do is work on your WHY. Years ago this Why concept was alien to me, some people call it a DREAM, others call it a REASON, whatever you want to call it, you've got to really know why you want to do what you want to do!

MY INTRODUCTION INTO THE WHY CONCEPT

I remember it was 1992, when my cousin Kay, out of the blue called me and told me someone wanted to speak with me. Little did I know my life was about to change as I heard him pass the phone over, and the voice at the other end said "Hello Philip, my name is Simon! I was just having a conversation with your cousin with regards to business and I asked him if he knew any sharp individuals that would be interested in a business opportunity."

Here I was a 22 year old hiding in college. Yes hiding, hiding because I really didn't want to go to college. To be honest with you, I found it boring, but who could I say that to? Who would be sympathetic to any suggestion that college might be boring, especially in a family where everyone had degrees in this and that, and where without a matriculation gown and hat you were not considered to have proven yourself fit to be called a human being.

I have always said one day I'll own my own business, but ask me what sort or how? I didn't have any idea of what and how, but alas here was somebody asking me if I was interested in a business opportunity? Of course I said yes, and agreed to meet him the following Monday. It was Friday night and I remember I couldn't sleep all weekend. I simply couldn't wait to see what this opportunity was all about, finally Monday arrived, I got to my cousin's flat early, I just couldn't contain my curiosity.

This gentleman walked in dressed in the sharpest suit I had ever seen and here I was dressed in my smartest outfit, which comprised of a shirt from Mr Byrite which was the Primark back then, a pair of trousers and my prized possession; my charcoal and white LA Gear trainers. Simon said, "Philip I have come to share a business idea with you but before I go into the details, I'd like to ask you what you want out of life?" That question rocked my world to the core.

What do I want out of life? What do I want? Out of life? Nobody ever asked me what I wanted. All I had heard all my life was what was expected of me, what my parents expected, what my friends wanted, what my teachers required, what the government demanded, nobody ever cared what I really desired, nobody, ever!

Here I was for the first time in my life asked by another human being what is it I really want? Instantly my brain started creating new synapses, pathways started forming in the realm of possibility when Simon interjected, "what kind of house would you like to buy and live in?" I thought, me, house? He continued without breaking his stride, "yes what car would you like to drive?" I was now recovering from my initial state of bewilderment, and realizing very quickly I better catch on right now or I will appear a fool to this gentleman. So I heard myself saying I would like a 3 bedroom house, that's as large as I could think of at that time!

Simon asked "are you sure. Why not go for a 5 bed roomed house?" That blew my mind again; you mean

I could legally dream of a 5 bed house? Am I allowed? Looking back now I am so grateful Simon spent 30mins dream building with me, what cars I liked, what colour, leather interior, what colour of leather? Could I smell the leather? On and on it went... The experience made me decide, I didn't care what this gentleman was into, I was in! Where do I sign?

DREAM BIG

"If the dream is big enough the facts don't count". Author Unknown

Why dream? If you want to do anything in life, you have to have motivation. Let's break that word down, Motive, Action. Motive for action! Your dream is your Motive for Action. The bigger your dream the bigger your motive for action! The bigger your dream the more you will find it impossible to procrastinate.

Look at it this way; in the physical world every object has a magnetic pull, the bigger the object the greater the pull. That's why there is a Sun and a Moon. The Sun is such a big object that its gravitational pull keeps all the planets revolving around it. Thank God for that or there will be no life on this planet we call Earth!

The Earth in turn with its gravitational pull keeps the moon in its orbit, and keeps you and I from flying off into space, now just like the gravitational pull, the size off your dreams attract the tools, resources and people that will help make your dreams come true.

Develop a big dream; dream really, really big, as you are more likely to achieve those dreams because of the inherent pull present in every big dream. Many books have been written on this subject, I have read a lot of them and from my personal experience I found them all true. I found the bigger my goal, the more calculating I am. I'm less likely to show up late at events or to meet those that matter to my goal. If I was struggling to find time to devote to making things happen, that suddenly ceases to be a problem because I find myself, investing the time! I find myself less involved in time wasting activities.

My sense of urgency greatly increases and I find I'm more energized and focused. I wake up earlier than usual and find myself inspired with solutions; I suddenly have no more excuses only answers. Circumstances and opportunities that will help accomplish the goal seem to happen a lot more frequent.

We human beings can do anything if only our reason, our WHY is big enough. There have been amazing stories of people accomplishing superhuman feats when faced with impossible situations that trigger a tremendous WHY! Like the story of a mother and her son.

She left her son working under his truck; her son always fixed his truck, he's gifted like that. She was in the kitchen when she heard the sound; Crunch! She ran out to find her son trapped under the truck. The paramedics got to the scene wondering how a truck weighing more than a ton was lifted off the victim. The jack was twisted and unusable!

There was no one else around for miles; when asked how she did it, she said "I just did it, I don't how or what happened! When I saw the truck on my son, I can't describe what came over me; I just wanted the truck off my son!"

I guess her "Why" was so big! That her "how"; using her bare hands got the job done. When the reason (the why) is big enough the facts don't count.

The film John Q starring Denzel Washington also illustrates this point. Look for the film, its worth seeing.

I believe you've gotten the point by now... You can do the most amazing things if only your reason is big enough. So don't worry about the 'How to' concern yourself more with the 'Why to' because when you know 'Why' the 'How' always presents itself without fail.

EXPLORING THE 'WHY' CONCEPT FURTHER

The man that knows 'Why' will always employ the man that knows 'How'.

I have seen a lot of instances where people with lots of education end up working for people of little or no education; I believe those with great education prepare themselves in most cases to work for others. Most individuals who are highly developed in the 'How' can only operate in organizations, institutions or establishments created by others. Observations have shown very few can start their own ventures and sustain it hence they end up working for people who are well versed in the 'Why' department.

Autobiographies of people like Richard Branson and Bill Gates and many others are the best proof of this point. Richard Branson apparently dyslectic started his entrepreneurial journey as a kid, by the time he was a teenager he was running a magazine business, and not long after that a mail order business, the rest as they say is history. My question is how many people with a huge amount of education work for him? Probably hundreds or thousands; my point is the lack of a high level of education has not been a hindrance to him. Here is a case of someone very early in life quickly identifying he's strength, maximizing it and employing people to deal with what he's not so good at! That folks; is wisdom in colour.

Bill Gates apparently from a middleclass family dropped out of college and went after his dream of Windows, its obvious today that he is one of the richest men in the world, his dropping out of high school hasn't been an issue, and some might even say it was a smart move he made. His dream of making the computer available to all was made possible not because of his education but he's entrepreneurial prowess laced with bravery.

In the book 'Think and Grow Rich' a story is told about Henry Ford. Henry Ford apparently wasn't an educated man in terms of academic knowledge; he was however very educated in the 'Why' aspect of things; developing the faculties of his mind to use the knowledge of the experts around him.

A newspaper called him an 'ignorant pacifist.' Henry Ford taking offense sued the paper for libel. For their defense the newspaper hired a lawyer who kept asking Henry Ford questions in an attempt to prove to all present that Henry Ford was in fact an illiterate! The lawyer rained a barrage of questions on current affairs, history, politics, economics and many other subject matters. Henry Ford apparently was not able to answer any of these questions. The defense Lawyer was just about to rest his case when, Henry Ford interrupted him, addressing the Lawyer he said, "may I remind you that on my desk I have a row of electric push buttons and if I really need answers to any of these questions you are asking, all I need to do is push one of those buttons, which would summon to my aid men that would furnish me with the answer to whatever question I desire!"

He proceeded to ask the court what use it would be to clutter his mind with general knowledge for answering questions, when he has men around him that would supply him answers to any question on any subject.

This response apparently floored the defense Lawyer, and proved to all present that this was not the response of an ignorant or illiterate man but of a person of great intellect. Those awake to the 'Why' concept like Henry Ford, understand it is better to use their mind for thinking, than use it as a library for general knowledge and trivial indulgences.

THE WHY CONCEPT IN A RAPIDLY CHANGING WORLD

In today's world business climate, those who can use their minds for creative, innovative, groundbreaking ideas and solutions rule. I call them the 'Why people.' Education is important however for education to continue to be relevant to today's world's demands; it has to be heavy on the 'Why' side of the equation to balance the 'How' knowledge that has too long been the focus of the world's learning culture.

Chapter 2

Mind Set

"He, who thinks of limitations, creates them"
-Anonymous-

If you want to change your world, you definitely need to work on your mind set.

Your mind set is the control centre of your world. It dictates who you are, and it sets the boundaries of what you think you can or cannot do. Just like a thermostat is to a powerful boiler; regardless of how powerful a boiler is, the thermostat dictates how hot or cold the output of the boiler will be.

Your mind set is like the thermostat. You will not achieve beyond what your mind has set.

Our mind set is informed by a host of things like our environment, background, sensory and extra sensory stimuli i.e. what we see, hear, touch or say. It is shaped by what we watch on the television, what kind of music we listen to, what kind of friends we keep and that which influences them plus the added issue of the kind of culture we originate from.

Whatever you feed your mind will undeniably shape your world.

Years ago I was of a mind set that I was just a boy, didn't know much, didn't have much and if I didn't take heed I will not become much! Today I am of a completely different mind set. I can do anything; achieve anything I want and more. What is more I am special and utterly unique. All I need to employ if I want to do anything is just to decide on it and it is as good as done. No excuses. No exceptions.

These are two entirely different mind sets and both in one human experience – my experience. One mindset made me completely unsure of myself and the other, utterly and irrevocably sure of what I am capable of achieving. What happened that changed me? Or more precisely how did I change?

Well I had to start with understanding what was informing my mind set. While I wouldn't change my childhood for all the wealth in the world, I discovered after careful study of my background that there were so many erroneous programming and running scripts in the dark recesses of my mind. This conscious and subconscious programming and diverse information had to be challenged and scrutinized for their validity.

Consciously:

Always do what you are told… Accept everything your elders say… Don't question things… Older folks are always right… Always tow the line… Traditions must always be followed. Don't keep eye contact with Adults!

Subconsciously:

Don't rock the boat… Don't volunteer for anything… Don't take responsibility for anything, have a give me, give me outlook in life… the majority are always right... Always be late as it is fashionable, on and on it goes. While some of the things highlighted above, like "always do what you are told!" were good for my safety while I was a child, nobody corrected that programming as I grew up into an adult, "Accept everything your elders say!" again good for my childhood, however I found many instances where doing that would just be fatal. This kind of programming are recipes for disaster in adulthood as one has to assimilate into other cultures. More on this in the chapter 'sign of the times'.

Take "Don't keep eye contact" for example; while in Nigeria that was believed shows respect, importing that mindset to England is fatal, why? Obviously over here, if you can't keep eye contact; you are seen to be shifty, hiding something, untruthful, not trust worthy. Try getting a job while you come across like that and find that success will be unattainable. The same goes when law enforcement officers are in the course of their duties and you come across like that; they are forced to believe that you must be guilty hence, your inability to keep eye contact. I believe many people are in jail for something as simple as running their lives on these ill fitting mindsets.

Your mindset is the sum total of what you are. It makes or breaks you. It is your worst enemy or your very best friend, it's that powerful.

Destructive Mindsets

What we all have to realize is; our mind is so powerful! So powerful that it literally creates for us whatever we want. I read this somewhere I can't remember where but it stuck in my mind:

"Whatever the mind sees it considers, whatever the mind does not consider it dismisses! What ever the mind continually considers it believes and whatever the mind continually believes it eventually does." The premise here is this 'I believe so therefore I become as I believe'.

What our mind doesn't do is differentiate between what we want and what we don't want; it just creates what images we feed it - through our mouths, eyes, ears and actions. In other words at the subconscious level our minds doesn't know fact from fiction, or that we don't really mean this or that, it just creates.

For example if you say something seemingly harmless like, I am always forgetful, if you keep saying that, you will believe it and before you know it you will always forget your keys, names, birthdays. This is truth!

What I have found is if you change those words from "I am always forgetful" to "I am never forgetful" and you keep saying it, your mind will eventually create that, and you will find yourself always remembering things and in your new reality you will not experience losing keys, forgetting names or birthdays and much more. So like I have had to learn, I don't say what I don't want because I realize my mind is always listening and if I don't want something negative I had better be disciplined enough in my speech not to say negative things that appear harmless on the surface but create havoc when manifested.

You and I know people that experience the doom and gloom where things always seem to go wrong for them. Now we know why! They are the ones the bailiff raided their house, broke their leg, got made redundant, have a neighbour from hell and just got struck by lightning! For them their mindset is stuck on the perception that 'things are really ok only when things go wrong'. When you have a conversation with such people, they believe all nature is out to get them. Remember what was said about the subconscious mind, it doesn't differentiate fact from fiction, and now let's see how they create their own world.

They say things like "I'm just unlucky" "bad things always seek me out" but you watch them, they keep saying that and sure enough when something supposedly bad happens, like they get up in the morning and the car doesn't start, they say I told you these things always happen to me! They forget that it has probably happened to millions of people that very morning, however because their focus is 'something bad always happens to me' they have just reaffirmed their mindset with its perceived negativities.

Someone else with a positive mindset would handle the same situation differently and get a totally different reality from this same set of circumstances. With an 'I am always fortunate mindset' they get to their car find out its not working and immediately rather than thinking 'o poor me' they think this is interesting I wonder what good is about to happen because when things seemingly inconvenient like this happen, I always, due to the delay experience something I would have missed if my car started. So this person is now on the look out for a positive experience. Is it any wonder this person now meets an old friend with whom they've lost contact with for years at a petrol station? Their paths wouldn't have crossed had the car started on time; thereby reinforcing their mindset that every time they experience an inconvenience something good is about to happen!

Back to our friends with "I'm just unlucky", "bad things always seem to happen to me" mindset.

What I have found is that even when good things start happening for them, their mindset says 'This isn't right!' and then proceed to find every way to sabotage their run of good fortune and when it finally succeeds, it sends a message to their world 'ok things are back to how they should be' you and I then hear them let out a sigh of relief; 'things are back to normal'. This as you can see cannot be considered healthy by any rational and sensible human being.

As you can see in the last example the negative thinking person was so convinced that bad things should happen to them, until it did! They were then able to say "see I told you, I'm always unlucky." Truth is they are the planner, architect and builder of their own misfortune.

The good news is; just as we can orchestrate misfortune with our minds, we can also create opportunity, wealth, good health, good relationships and any other thing we desire with our minds.

ATTITUDE: A GREAT TOOL FOR CHANGING YOUR WORLD

Having the right attitude is an amazing weapon in the quest of changing your world. Smile instead of frowning, compliment instead of complaining, encourage instead of criticizing, always have something good to say about everything. Add to things instead of being a drain. Give of yourself willingly and enthusiastically and your world can not remain gloomy and dark. Have a good attitude towards yourself, your close relatives, your friends, your acquaintances, your work colleagues, your job (This one could require a lot of discipline), your neighbourhood, your city, your government, your country! Why? The truth is, that's all you've got! If you have a bad or negative attitude towards all you've got, what chance have you got?

You start smiling and watch people smile back! You start encouraging people and watch people encourage you back; you start complimenting people and watch people start reciprocating. You start saying good things about everything and you'll notice everyone around you stop saying negative things; they will start saying good things about you and things around you will be good. You start adding to things rather than being a drain and watch people flock to you. You start being enthusiastic about life and watch people bring opportunities your way, you continue to give of yourself expecting nothing back and watch people start supporting anything concerning you.

Changing your world is simple; I didn't say it is easy! A lot of these things I suggest you do might not come naturally to you or be straightforward, you've just got to do what works, and by so doing you are able to change your world. THIS WORKS! 'How to win friends and influence people' by Dale Carnegie is a wonderful book that will help in this area.

IT TAKES TIME

When you decide to change your world, don't expect it to happen in a day. You are effectively revealing a new you to the world. The world has known you a certain way, so when you try to change your resolve will be tested.

I remember when I first started to smile, imagine this I'm a 6ft 2inches black skinned guy from Nigeria, I flashed a smile to a stranger who happened to be a white chap and this poor guy nearly jumped out of his skin. I probably came across so odd, my body language was probably one of apprehension because I was doing what I wasn't yet used to. Trying to do new things will offer some comical moments to remember. Don't shy away from attempting the new. You will be better for it.

It took a while of determination and persistence before I started seeing the fruit of my new actions. Today when I smile, people pay me compliments, we become acquainted and most of the times become good friends, doing this I have friends from all over the world, that's one of the beauty of living in London. The whole world is here! White, Black, Chinese, Indian, Eastern European; everyone is my friend because I learnt how to smile, which made me approachable.

Can you not see how doing these things cannot but change your world? Why not commit to trying these strategies, and start to change your world. Try it! Things might just work for you!

When you start speaking good about everything, people will watch you, and will even draw you into arguments or gossip, just to test your resolve, you will have to learn as I did, how to politely state that you are not going to be negative about anything or anybody, and boldly make it known that you don't mind if you will be labeled, weird, Looney, or weak! When people see you are ready to go all the way with your new reality, they will either accept you or they will back off!

WHAT HAPPENS WHEN BAD THINGS HAPPEN?

We can't always choose what happens to us but we can always choose how we respond to it. You are driving along minding your own business, you spotted the sign on the road you are driving on is marked 30miles per hour, so you keep within the speed limit, suddenly you have an apparently impatient driver tail gating you, looming in your rear view mirror, driving menacingly up from your rear, honking, making hand gestures implying you are a low life! What do you do? A, let him understands he's a lunatic? B, Make sure he doesn't get away with terrorizing folks on the road or C, prefer for him go on his merry way with the assumption he didn't spot that he's in a 30miles an hour zone, and he's probably a good guy if you get to know him?

I personally have tried A, made sure he knows he's a lunatic. What I found however is after I have finished making my hand gestures allowing my blood to boil, on hindsight it's always hard to remember what the big deal was. So I have learnt to stop choosing 'A'. How about you?

I have also tried B; I have never liked bullies so it suddenly becomes my mission in life that when I see such incidences, I jump right in. I have learnt this isn't smart either!

Because I can't imagine road rage perpetrators and victims woke up that day thinking 'Today, I'll smash someone on the head with my wheel spanner, that'll teach them not to mess with me!' 'I won't mind being led off to jail in handcuffs for murder, I won't mind 15 seconds of madness destroying my entire life, destroying my family and robbing me of all my potential'.

I bet they don't start the day thinking that. Or the victim, waking up that day having a yawn and a good stretch thinking to themselves, 'I think it'll be a good idea today; to get involved in a road dispute, get my head smashed in with a wheel spanner!' 'That'll be a great present for my family, dying at a road rage incident isn't a bad idea!' It just isn't a smart thing to get involved in, either as the aggressor or the victim; the best thing I have found to do is C, choose to let them go on their merry way! I wouldn't want to kill anyone; neither do I want to be killed by anyone.

The quality of our life is solely dependent on the quality of our choices, so make the right choices.

With the right attitude we can always choose how we accept any circumstance. Many bad and negative things can happen at anytime; death of a loved one, losing a job, relationship breakdown, anything under the Sun! What I have realized is that these things hurt, and some really, really hurt that it threatens to kill us, however I have also learnt that there is good in every and any circumstance we find ourselves, no matter how hard it is to find!

Before you write me off as an idealist and probably on a designer drug, let me explain further. My brothers and I said goodnight to my Dad, we had a normal night sleep to wake up in the morning to find my Father dead! He had died during the night! My youngest brother slept right beside him. Thankfully I had trained my mind to see the good in everything. I observed him, saw he had a blissful expression on his face. I realized he didn't struggle in passing away! My brother sleeping next to him and not noticing anything was another proof! I thought to myself, even in this bad circumstance I was thankful he died in bed; many are not that fortunate, many are scraped off the roads dying in car accidents. So I was thankful, and I pray when my time comes I go as peaceful as he went. I realized he had run his race, he had finished his course he has now passed the baton to us his children, all 6 of us. So I rejoiced in the life he lived and vowed right there in that room, silently to myself that we won't let him down.

Your mindset takes orders from you the possessor of your mind.

Now there were so many other ways I could have decided to respond to such an experience. I could have thrown myself on the floor, claimed witches and wizards have succeeded in killing our father, proceed to blame everyone around for not doing this or that, I could have been part of the problem, but I chose differently. I chose to turn that potentially destructive experience into an empowering one.

I am so thankful God has given us all the ability to turn every adversity into a victorious advantage. Turning Jesus Christ's death on the cross to an ultimate victory is final proof; every circumstance can be accepted as defeat or victory! The choice is ours.

Again the quality of our life is dependent on the quality of our choices.

YOU TALK TO YOURSELF

Self talk is another great tool in changing your world; for many years I wasn't aware that I talk to myself, we all do! If you know nothing about this concept I can appreciate how that sounds to you, for the next few sentences just bear with me and keep an open mind. To help me help you hear yourself please…

Say this out loud. "I am a winner!"

If you have not done this before it will feel really weird, but let's put that aside for the moment.

Say it out loud again. "I am a winner!"

You will hear yourself agreeing or disagreeing with what you've just said! Congratulations you've just heard yourself talk to yourself.

Now if your mind set is the thermostat your self talk is the dial. I realized the importance of correcting the forever running commentary in the background of my mind. My self talk I found was a major key for me to correct my mind set. I watch what I say, I never say I can't, or I'll try, I replace my self talk with "I can" and "I will". As you can see, if I say "I can't" then with my own self talk I have set the dial of my mindset to – 'make it impossible for me to do!'.

Stop saying things like "it's impossible, it won't work, I am bad luck", or say things like "I am so stupid" when you make mistakes, purge your vocabulary of all negative words, sentences and expressions. Your subconscious is always listening and it takes in everything literally and creates your world with what it takes in good or bad!

Try this! Listen to your own words for at least a month, a lot of us think we know ourselves while the truth is, for most people; we haven't even met ourselves yet! Take note of everything you say, scrutinize them, then imagine you are outside yourself listening to yourself! If you met yourself, the only thing, you can judge yourself with are your words; how would you describe you?

Books like, “The Magic of Thinking Big” “Think and Grow Rich “and “How to win friends and influence people” were tremendously helpful in helping me correct my erroneous mindset.

I realized I was making progress, when my self talk finally matched the running commentary in the background of my mind. Earlier on in my journey whenever I said out loud, I AM A WINNER! My mind would reply –“no you are not!”, and it will proceed to give me instances and reasons why I am not a winner. If that is where you are don’t despair, because as time went on and I kept saying positive things about myself, kept using empowering self talk instead of defeatist ones. I can’t say the exact day it happened, however one day I said, I AM A WINNER! And amazingly I heard my mind come back with YES YOU ARE!!! I was amazed, I tried it again and it came back with the same response. WOW!

In life, the only objections you really have to overcome are your own!

When your mindset agrees with your positive self talk, you have now started to change your world; you are now in the position of power. Your confidence will sky rocket, and your world will respond accordingly, like dropping a pebble in a body of water, the ripple effect will resonate in all areas of your life.

A LITTLE ON COMFORT ZONES

Consciously and unconsciously we operate confined within the parameters set by our minds, we all have comfort zones; these are areas of our life where we feel we are in control, where we genuinely feel confident. Take speaking in public for example, some people's worst nightmare is to speak publicly, they freeze! Their voice starts shaking, they suddenly develop sweaty palms but speak to them one on one, they now speak eloquently and with ease.

While speaking in public they are out of their comfort zone - operating outside the parameters set by their mind, speaking one on one is not a problem for them as it is within the preset parameters of their mind so they feel ok. Now with what we know about mindsets and self talk; we can extend our comfort zones to cover things we would normally feel uncomfortable with.

Still using the public speaking example, let's say you are having difficulty with public speaking, you can start changing your world by saying "I am a wonderful public speaker," "people always love hearing me speak!"

"I always know what to say and never freeze..." if you continue with such positive self talk and never give up, you will find the next time you speak in public you will find it easier, the more you do it the better you become.

Apply this method to other areas of your life, where you believe you could do with some improvements.

People see me today, they see a self assured confident person, and some people wrongly believe I was born this way; that couldn't be further from the truth. I changed my world by extending my comfort zones using self talk.

This I believe you will find is another powerful tool in changing your world - extending your comfort zones.

Imagine the potential we all have in us to be released by constantly expanding and extending our comfort zones? We are truly amazing beings and the only one of God's creations that can exercise these life changing truths. What's more, with these truths we can start changing our world right away!

My question to you is why not start right now?

Why not start changing your world right away?

Chapter 3

Sign of The Times

"Most people don't recognize opportunity because it is usually dressed in overalls and it looks like work"
-Author unknown-.

We have looked at the importance of Why and the Mindset in our quest to change your world now its time to know what time it is!

Sign of the Times…

PARADIGM SHIFTS

What is a Paradigm? A paradigm is any accepted dogma concerning any subject which has cemented over time. There was a time the accepted dogma was that the earth was flat, and as ridiculous as this may sound to us now, man believed if he traveled far enough in one direction he would eventually fall off the earth! When some men started to notice, just by observation, that the earth was showing signs of being round, some other men saw that as a threat to their accepted dogma. They saw this new information as propagated by trouble makers; history has always shown men to resent other men who seem to want to "rock the boat."

Men that chose not to ignore the signs because of 'accepted dogma' have down through the ages been hailed as visionaries and pioneers! They enjoyed the success that came from standing by their convictions; despite the overwhelming resistance of the majority.

At the turn of the century, the industrial revolution was just getting in its stride; taking over from the Agricultural based economy. At that time everyone was involved in some kind of enterprise; entrepreneurial families gave themselves family names that reflected what services they offered. Names like Smith, in the blacksmith and silversmith industry, Tailor; the tailoring business, The Butchers, Farmers and so on.

People like Andrew Carnegie, Thomas A. Edison, and Henry Ford spoke about the dawn of a new age, where industry would usher in mass production and drive down the cost and time of producing everything. Henry Ford dreamt of building a car that the common man could afford, for at that time only the very rich could afford cars because it took months even in some cases over a year to make one car. Henry Ford promised he would run assembly lines that would make a car in minutes; at that time people were sure he was a lunatic. History proves them wrong and good old Henry's Legacy is still very much part of our everyday life, think about that next time you spot a car with the Ford logo.

Naturally industry required lots and lots of people so there was a mass recruitment drive, remember every family had a business, so while industry sought to fill its ranks with people, it encountered resistance from the likes of Mr. Farmer who forbade his children from leaving the farm for the industry. As far as Mr. Farmer was concerned his father was a farmer, his grandfather was a farmer and by heck his son is going to be a farmer as well!

Others took the risk and went into industry and industry had a lot to invest in them, not the least loads of MONEY! When they came back home they had been paid hefty salaries, a company car, and loads of perks, country club membership and subsidized beautiful homes for all their trouble. What do you think Mr. Farmer's son did when they saw their contemporaries with all these trappings of a good life, while all they had was subsistence off their family land? Of course, everyone left the land and family businesses and looked for a job!

A paradigm shift occurred! The world moved from an Agricultural based existence to an Industrial based one.

Universities became big business because industry required skills, like accountancy, medicine, engineering, physicists, chemists, lawyers, hence was born the partnership as time went on between Universities and Industries. Around the 1930s onwards people where interested in which University you went to and what qualification you achieved.

A University degree became a license to print money...

The industrial revolution ruled. It ruled so long that it became the accepted dogma. The mantra every parent taught their child was; go to school, get your degree and get a 'good job'. And who could blame them? The evidence was overwhelming, those with degree faired well for so long that they just could not see another paradigm shift on the horizon. Enter the computer revolution!

The signs were there but the majority could not read them. Through hind sight I can remember in the late 1980s when the first slow down of job availability for university graduates became evident.

Industries that always relied on manpower switched more and more into automation, machines started replacing humans in the work place, and they were a lot more efficient, less expensive to run (You don't have to pay for holidays) and Reliable (They don't go on strikes). The human displacement got worse in the 90s, it was glaring! Before the 1990s there was something called 'a job for life' but by the end of the 1990s just 10 short years there was no longer a single job that could be labeled 'for life'! How's that for a paradigm shift? That's how fast these shifts can happen.

As far as I can recall I can't remember people on the streets screaming "Watch out; things are changing we are experiencing a paradigm shift!" I can't remember it been said on the news! Or at the work place, all you saw was the silent, gradual evidence of university graduates coming out of universities with wide eyed expectation of success, silently and gradually becoming disillusioned. They attend many, many interviews, 6 months go by, 1 year, 2, 3 years then it finally dawns on them they had better settle for a security job, stacking shelves or the check out till at Sainsbury's, Tescos, Asda or any of the other retail outlets.

THE LEGACY OF THE INDUSTRIAL REVOLUTION

While the industrial revolution changed our world and brought with it many outstanding contributions, it also brought with it an over reliance on institutions, governments and companies. Because it was around for nearly a century, many people weren't prepared for the changes that would hit our world. They had so designed their lives around the premise that jobs would take care of them for life. Governments can never fail them (Pensions) that they couldn't see what was coming. As such they stuck to the mantra "go to school, get a good job and do that for the rest of your life and you'll be fine."

The reality we see today shows that to be so far from the truth. And that folks, is frightening!

It is now common knowledge that if you are under 35 years old, you are deluding yourself on a grand scale if you are looking forward to a state or company funded pension. With nothing like a job for life, the notion of a career is obsolete, why? Because the average person is expected to change jobs at least 7 times in their life time. In today's business world, loyalty to employees is seen as unnecessary. Competition is rife as there are more people than there are jobs, because machines displacing manpower from industry hasn't stopped, in fact it has increased at a tremendous and unrelenting rate. Man like never before continues to be faced with not being needed by commerce and industry.

Think about that the next time you use an ATM machine or use the self check-out facility at your local supermarket.

Another thing we are seeing happen is commerce and industry going to countries with the cheapest labour, nowadays when I get a call from BT its usually from a call centre in India! And they do a very good job! Banks have moved their customer services to countries where people are prepared to work 24hrs if need be and get paid a fraction of what a British or American worker would demand.

Not to forget the effects of the European Union, people from most parts of Europe have a right to compete for jobs in England, and compete they do, being ready to work for very low pay and still do outstanding jobs.

As you can see today's worker is fighting for survival in a war on too many fronts.

This folks are the signs of the times…

To change your world you've got to know what time it is!

Too many people are going about their daily lives oblivious to the changes going on around them; totally unprepared to take advantage of the opportunities in a fast changing world. One thing is certain you cannot carry on with a business as usual outlook, if you are, you are already left behind. In a world of rapid change, you need not to be only good at dealing with change; you need to be good at anticipating the changes so that you can place yourself at the right place, at the right time.

To illustrate an example of a rapid change, not too long ago there was an IT boom! I can remember this time vividly. Everyone was suddenly in the IT industry. Professionals like Accountants, Lawyers, Bankers and people from all works of life catapulted themselves head long into the IT industry attracted by amazing salaries, 250,000 per year, and contractors earned even more. Everyone I met was into IT, Java was the craze, and I was 'advised' by several people to follow this apparent cash cow. Fortunately by then I was already exposed to information on paradigm shifts, so I kept my cool, even when I saw people buying cars and houses, I stuck with my suspicion that all wasn't as it seemed. The bubble had to burst.

It went on for 2 or 3 more years then suddenly it peaked, gradually salaries offered began dropping, and dropping before long the same jobs that were paying £70,000 a month, started paying less than 20 grand per annum. My suspicion was right it was a flash in the pan boom that quickly dissipated. It was obvious that everyone thought the IT revolution was going to bring back a huge demand for man power like the industrial revolution did, they were wrong! It unfortunately didn't.

Like I said earlier the days of pinning our hopes on industries, companies and even governments taking care of our futures are long gone.

THE ENTERPRENURIAL AGE

Instead of hoping industries, companies and governments will take care of us, these are times we have to realize that; we create new industries, companies, and we take care of governments. It will always be ok to have a job temporarily; however we all have to put more of ourselves into being innovative, being creative and developing our own unique abilities. The market is no longer crying out for employees, it is crying out for employers. It is crying out for new ways of thinking, creative ways of solving problems, the market is more and more interested in ground breaking ideas on how to create things quicker, better and cheaper.

If you want to be wealthy in this age you have to be good in either creating new stuff, or good in distributing new stuff to the market place.

Some people still hope being a good employee will cut it, being a good employee is worth nothing nowadays, why? Because employers want to know what you as an employee are directly bringing to the bottom line, 'Profit' of the company. If the company can make 180,000 per year from your a personal effort, of cause they don't mind paying you 18,000 per year as a thank you. However in contrast if by employing you, your personal effort only generates 18,000 or less and you earn 18,000 per annum; unfortunately you are not needed. You are a liability.

DON'T DESPAIR!

There is always a temptation to despair at the rapidly changing world and the personal changes we have to make to excel. What we must always remember is opportunity is always found where ever chaos is. These are truly exciting times, if you desperately hold on to the past you will miss the opportunity to change your world. Let go! Just let go. Have you noticed you can't receive anything with your hand clenched? So just let go, let go of plans that require old thinking to achieve, thinking like "I will get a job and stay there for 45years and then retire on a pension" Let it go. That is not going to happen anymore in this world ever!

Let go of the notion that the majority must be right! Or there is safety in numbers, believing in that in today's world is futile. Ask those who experienced the dot com crash, those who have been made redundant from big, huge companies, 911 and with America's might, and the mess that the world is watching unfold. No, I personally don't find safety in numbers; too many people follow too many people to their doom! Whenever I see too many people going in one direction; alarm bells start going off! For me I do not subscribe to the tribe mentality in this case.

Unfortunately too many people are content and comfortable allowing the majority to think for them, decide for them, and take care of them. They are very quick to surrender their own judgment to the media, the government and their next door neighbour.

RUN! RUN!! RUN!!!

Picture this scenario if you will…

The scene is of a normal street. A few people going about their normal day to day business, when suddenly one individual appears startled, he jumps and instantly takes off running in one direction. He's overall expression is that of obvious horror and this is perceived by everyone in the vicinity. What happens? The next person imagining danger takes off running in the direction of apparent safety.

Seeing two people take off; now the third person takes a hurried glance in the opposite direction to see what's chasing them, but not wanting to risk his life or waste time he runs after the first two. Now three people are running, and a fourth person follows suit. Eventually, five people running in one direction has confirmed to everyone the need to run! run!! run!!! At this point fear and flight take over which now produces a stampede of people speeding in one direction.

Everyone is now running but nobody knows why, at least not yet! Let's ask the guy at the back of the pack,

'Why are you running sir?'

'I don't know!' he says, but breathing heavily he adds, 'we must be running from something, look at all the people running.' He darts off trying to keep up.

Catching up with him, he points ahead to a lady running in her high heels.

The same fellow blurts out, 'She looks like she knows why we are running; in fact she must know'. In the melee she is approached,

'Hello lady', "Hello" she says short of breath, 'Why are you running? She is asked. 'Why! Can't you see what is chasing us?' She hurriedly answers.

'No'is the answer, followed by the enquiry, 'Can you tell us what's chasing all of you?' "No" says the lady, as she adds, 'I just know it's something bad'. She continues to run as fast as she can.

Things that make you go Hmmm. Ok, let's cut to the chase and ask the guy that started all this running in the first place. 'Sir, why are you running? Though tired he has a certain determination as he begins, 'I'm running to catch my friend before he leaves home. He's travelling today and I have just noticed that I have his passport, I mistakenly picked it up with my books when I was packing my briefcase this morning.' he explains with a concerned expression.

I know I might be guilty of over caricaturing this scenario, but you grasp what I'm getting at.

THE HERD MENTALITY

Nature has blessed us with the instinct of fear and flight, but for you to change your world, you must discipline this instinct. Begin to educate and master your emotions. The widely held notion that the majority is always right must in part always be questioned by you, and, if you must feel fear and run, then you must at least know why.

GOLD RUSH! DIAMOND RUSH!

The gold rush and the diamond rush are examples of our innate tendency to rush blindly. There was a time in history, 1849 to be precise, in the American state of California, someone found gold! And to help things move along, apparently, shortly thereafter, another man ran down the street holding a bottle filled with gold dust shouting Gold! Gold! Gold! What do you think happened after that? A stampede of course! Prospectors came from all corners of the globe to stake their claim. History records that though there was gold, sadly, very few became wealthy.

Eighteen years after, in Southern Africa diamonds were discovered. The stampede from all over the world again descended on South Africa, people seeking their fortune. Historians proved yet again that very few individuals actually made their fortune.

I will tell you the people that really became wealthy, whilst the others scrambled at the call of gold or diamonds. Those that achieved great wealth were the ones who saw the people rush for the gold or diamond, but understood that beyond the gold or diamond, there was a far greater opportunity in providing goods and services for the miners and prospectors. The people that sold food, made a mint. The people selling liquor couldn't stop money flowing into their coffers. As for those in the accommodation, entertainment, even the protection business (Security) industry made far more money overall than the gold or the diamond dealers.

I am not against rushing. If one must rush; rush armed with information, rush with a plan, rush with an overall strategy and a personal philosophy.

THE WAY OF THE CONTRARIAN

To embrace responsibility and change in a rapidly changing world will increasingly require a contrarian spirit. A contrarian goes against the grain, swims against the tide and travels the opposite direction to the horde. From the root word 'contrary', a contrarian does things contrary to the norm, never follows the crowd, observes and makes decisions based not on the overwhelming conclusion of the masses, but on the overwhelming conclusion of his or her own personal convictions.

The way of the contrarian is usually the way of a pioneer.

As a contrarian one must learn to go on without the approval and acceptance of the majority, one must not expect applause or encouragement from the masses. This spirit, in its entirety forges along the road less travelled. It is a scary adventure that promises a tremendous amount of benefits.

The rewards are apparent, as it always happens after the hordes have gone in one direction (the herd mentality syndrome!), which leaves the contrarians to enjoy the green pastures left behind. While the majority fight continuously over limited resources, contrarians enjoy the benefits of not having to compete for resources, because of cause people are usually not focused in their direction. While people feel safe because they are doing what everyone else is doing, a contrarian feels uneasy for that very fact. Safety for a contrarian is always in doing what nobody else thinks is viable on so many levels. The contrarian has a sixth sense and behaves likewise. A contrarian learns to trust his or her own judgment and runs with it. Why not you stir up that contrarian spirit within you, it will equip you better for the new reality of entrepreneurism that the world is moving into.

Chapter 4

Design Your World

"If you don't design your world, it will be designed for you by default."
-Mr. Phil-

Have you ever asked yourself why there is a rush hour in the mornings and evenings? Society has designed people's lives to run a certain way, so much so they can't live without the design. In London, around 5am in the morning the routine starts, first cleaners make the daily pilgrimage to the City, they clean everything, if you don't get out of their way you will be swept into a dust pan and dumped into a bin! Just joking! Around 7am they all leave the City and then the office workers now make their own daily pilgrimage.

About noon everyone goes for Lunch and around 5pm they start making their way out of the City to their respective homes. If you travel on the tube - you study people. Anyone who is fortunate enough to get a seat wears a gloomy face – I call it the 'Tube face'! Those who find themselves standing carry the demeanor of a convict because nobody wants to be there. Smiles are rare down there and eye contact not held for more than a fraction of a second. When you enter an empty coach watch how people sit; it's all predictable, someone sits here, the next person finds somewhere as far away from the first person, and that process is continued until people have no other choice but to sit next to someone, as soon as this the occurs then and only then does everyone now start to sit beside each other till the coach is full. All this happens in silence and devoid of interaction. It seems like the unsaid rule on the underground, alas, it appears that

People are like a herd driven by an invisible herdsman.

THE INVISIBLE HERDSMAN...

In our world we are so dependent on televised media. The general consensus is if it is on TV it must be true, right? - Wrong! Most people consciously or unconsciously get direction for their life from the TV. Whatever you listen to, watch and associate with shapes your world. Whether you agree with me or not, we are all programmed, and we can't escape it! Trying to escape it will be like trying to take a bath without getting wet. There are many examples of programming, I'll start with babies. The moment a child is born, programming starts; infants like to wake up at night when everyone is sleeping but with their parents programming, they eventually learn to sleep at night and play in the day time. This proofs that all patterns can be altered at will.

While we cannot stop programming from occurring, what we can all do is choose who does the programming. People can only do to you what you allow them to.

There are many forces in our world today that would gladly programme us if we let them, and that's the key 'If we let them'. Companies, governments and large consortiums selling products spend billions of pounds yearly to programme you and I through advertising. I'm not saying it is good or bad that's not my point here, my point is we all need to be aware when we are being programmed so that we can choose what programming we allow and which ones we disallow.

The day I started choosing my programming was the day I started changing my world.

There are good stuff out there and there are lethal stuff. The solution to balancing the equation is to wake up to our God given responsibility to choose right and not to allow filth and garbage to destroy our lives! Like the computer jargon 'GIGO' - Garbage in Garbage out! It goes without saying that what we put in our lives is what we'll get out of our lives. The mind is so powerful and it was not designed to switch off, even when you are asleep you are constantly taking in information, try it! If you go to bed listening to good soothing music, there is a great chance you will wake up relaxed and happy. Try leaving your TV on the Horror channel all night, chances are you will have a restless and disturbed pattern of sleep all night, after which you will wake up disgruntled, tired and irritated. It is time for us to be smart.

A plethora of media programmes the masses. Years ago I stopped watching the news religiously. I grew up watching my Dad watch the news religiously; he even believed it was healthy. I also believed that was the case until I started asking questions like why do they perpetually cover bad news? Why do they cover the same story over and over again from different angles to create an effect that things are worse than they are? There are 2 sides to any story, how can we make accurate judgments or an informed decision if we don't have access to the other side of the story? The most powerful men in the world now are not Presidents or Heads of State. The most powerful men are the Rupert Murdock's and Ted Turner's of this world. These are the media king pins who control the instrument of mass programming and subliminal persuasion.

I watch people get on with their lives secure in their assumption that the media would and should always have their best interest at heart! Is this really how it is? How naïve can we be to allow ourselves to be hoodwinked! Folks we've got to be smarter than that.

Television programmes like Eastenders, Coronation Street, Neighbours, Big Brother, Reality shows, and a host of Celebrity infused programmes I believe programme people for a life of mediocrity, failed marriages, extra-marital affairs and all manner of disastrous lifestyles.

Sometimes people try to defend these shows by saying its only depicting what is happening in real life. I feel like grabbing them by their shoulders and shaking some sense into them! The fact of the matter is, watching these shows programme people into thinking what they portray is indeed a type of lifestyle some people out there live, propagating these sort of things on Soap Operas locks in a self fulfilling prophesy, a self fulfilling prophesy which in the end guarantees the decay of the moral fibre of any individual and before long these things manifest in people's lives.

It has also been proven over extensive studies that the media spins a majority of its content to rouse and misinform the public for certain special interests, this undeniably affect individuals on deep personal levels. Believe this or not, you are being programmed by what you watch and listen to.

MTV as a media tool introduced music videos that inspired the young to declare a revolution that was at its core also lethal. Watching scantily clad girls swinging their hips, profanity, drug abuse and wanton excess can't be good programming! Why? Because it is sending out a false message about the world! These are some of those false messages; 'You have made it if you can sing,' 'Women are there for pleasure only,' 'if you have blinage you have arrived and if you don't you are nothing.' to site just a few. All these artists are or who purport to be rich, wealthy and financially sound are not. The sad truth is very much different to what the listening public are led to believe. For every artist that is on your screen there is someone in the background making the real bucks. Michael Jackson discovered this with his dealings with Sony, Diana Ross after many years in the industry finally wised up and advocated the importance of artists fully understanding the business side of the music industry; you can ask S club 7 the dangers of not heeding that advice. Prince had a highly publicized rift with his record moguls that for a long while he performed under a false name.

Closer study of music videos and Hollywood will reveal a strategy of painting a picture that life is about living in the fast lane, going around with your entourage in fancy cars and having pool side barbecues with nearly naked women stroking your face whilst pouting and purring at your being the man. Have you noticed that the women are always shamefully under clothed and the men are always fully clothed sometimes even abnormally over clothed! The colours and lighting sell us a lie that I personally wasn't exempt from buying into it, hook, line and sinker!

As for the music, oh my! Those beats that electrify the senses! They were and still are so bang on amazing, and what do they do? They open our conscious and subconscious minds to an almighty con. It's all a con and a deadly one at that, unfortunately. Not too different from the fairy tale of the Pied Piper of Hamelin.

Why is it a con? It is a con because what they portray is far from the truth (Reality). Let's take the virtually naked women, stroking your face while you are having a barbecue around the pool scenario, what bull! (Pardon my French) What?!

Is your girlfriend, fiancée, wife which ever one, ever and I mean ever, if you have a meaningful productive relationship; stroke your face with 6 other women beside any pool? Of course not, but we watch it and at some level if we are honest with ourselves, we even end up believing some people must live like that. The truth is even if you find someone that does have a life like that; I wouldn't wish it on anybody. Hugh Hefner and the girls of the Playboy mansion come to mind. Anyone with a discerning eye would see the pain, dysfunction and depravity that lurk under all the glamour. This is another form of programming.

SEEING THROUGH THE HYPE

The truth is that successful artist like P Diddy, Jay-Z and Snoop Dog are shockingly hard workers, smart workers and disciplined businessmen. When you see them dancing with models, yes models, if they danced with their real wives you wouldn't watch the video! Trust me! Swigging crystal and showing off amazing houses, cars and jewelry; they are at work. That's work for them; it is promotion for their new line of trainers, designer wear, and other business projects. While you might think that is life, they know it is business. You might be fooled, they certainly are not!

The uninformed who buy into the lies think that's how life is and ignore the real qualities that bring success. The fact remains that it is skills like becoming a good planner, a good dreamer, a good leader, having a disciplined producer, reading books, developing people skills, becoming an effective communicator, the list goes on and on. Television has become the greatest distraction the world has ever experienced. Distraction from the truth!

Do I watch TV? Yes I do! However I am now an informed viewer which means I don't watch what they want me to watch, I watch what helps me to be better at my craft! I take control. How do you take control? I will tell you what I do and then you can choose if it is useful for you. I never sit in front of the TV to see what's on. Channel surfing is a no-no and an invitation for being sucked into the vortex of the same vicious circle! I plan my day and use the TV guide to choose programmes of interest. I know channels that have productive and empowering content, channels like the History Channel, Discovery, Biography Channel, and Travel and leisure channels e.t.c. I never attempt to watch the TV without a plan, and regardless of what else that would try and distract me I commit myself to sticking with my plan. There are many channels and they vie for your attention with supposedly interesting things that if you are not careful the TV - the one eyed monster will eat you alive.

I look at the youth of today and perceive that their programming is coming from the TV, music videos, computer games, and the commercial world around them. The result is a disillusioned, detached and numb generation. They have been bombarded with such sensory overload to an extent that they have no choice but to be numb.

Their young minds can't see through the hype, but they know something isn't quite right hence, the angst that fills society! They've seen Mum and Dad struggle all their lives, Uncles, Aunties struggling.

They have been told the way to the good life is to do well in school, but they know things don't add up. What they see on TV doesn't match the reality they live. When they try to get answers from the people that should know, they are given the same old clichés that doesn't answer their questions, but leaves them still questioning themselves, their world and the people in it. It must be torture for these teenagers! Imagine living in a reality that is perpetually out of phase and a reality that will not own up to its actual state.

I observe the generations and I see the legacy of the Industrial age, the computer age and the information age. Those that grew up in the industrial age despite all the changes in the world and all the evidence to the contrary; still believe a job 'for life' is still the way to go. Those of the computer age are forever looking for the highest paying jobs that would make it all right, this keeps eluding them and you see them scratch their heads in confusion. To make matters worse Hollywood, the media and the system keep spewing out the programming to anesthetize everyone's pain. The pain is far from gone. Then you have the youth looking on and saying to themselves, if this is all we have to look forward to, we might as well have fun now! No wonder every adult complains that their teenager isn't listening to them! The result is a young population that is devoid of a purpose and the drive it needs to actualize it.

The answer I believe is in being responsible for our own programming.

'You will be the same as you are today save two things the people you meet and the books you read.' Author unknown

Earlier I pointed out that we are all programmed, I also pointed out that we can choose who does the programming. I strongly suggest you do your own programming. You see I realized my mind, your mind, our minds are immensely powerful and are the tools of creation; we can use it to build or destroy ourselves, in which ever case, it never fails to create. Start with the end in mind. Get a picture of the kind of life you want, pictures of cars, houses, get as detailed as you can about every aspect of your ideal life. What you are doing is giving your powerful mind (the tool of creation) materials with which to build.

Images are the material of the mind.

What ever you feed your eyes, what your ears constantly listen to, whatever your mouth says are the material your mind will use to create your world. If all you see constantly is death, lack, blood, pain then your world will be of death, lack, blood and pain. On the other hand if all you see are progress, joy, creativity and productivity; that will be your world. Control what you see, ear and say.

It isn't smart to allow negative filth in our minds and expect positive valuable things to come out.

Start reading books like, The Magic of thinking big, How to win friends and influence people, Think and Grow Rich. Reading is a must if you want to change your world. Reading changed my world; when we read, images are formed in our minds and those images expressed become our lives. Some people relegate reading to something they did in school, college or university and after graduating they believe reading is behind them. The fact is and I should know since I educated myself; after graduating is when real important reading begins. Education is not an event but a life-long process.

Let's think about it, universities are just places of learning with a set curriculum, most of this curriculum is to service commerce and industry. I see many people that have walked through the halls of academia and cannot form an original thought. They have been institutionalized and find it very hard to think outside that box. When I say reading I don't mean text books and going for more qualifications; I mean reading to expand your mind, your awareness and your world. Books like the ones I have stated above are a must read for someone serious about taking control and thinking freely. These books will lead you to others and there are literarily millions of books out there with profound information that'll blow your mind. The information that was not exposed in universities and other higher institutions lie in the people and literature that broke the molds of society itself. When you start delving into such matters you will wonder why they wasted your time for so long with near useless exertions. Intelligence is achieved through investing in you.

"When the student is ready the teacher appears." Author unknown

"Winners are readers and readers are winners."

If you don't learn something new everyday you are not growing, and anything in life that is not growing is dying. There is no standing still and maintaining and you cannot drift up the mountain. All of nature has been designed such that if it ceased from growing it starts dying; this is true for everything and anything under the sun. Think about it!

THE PEOPLE YOU MEET

The people you meet determine your direction in life; up or down. Parents charge their children to be alert about the friends they keep. There was a healthy fear regarding their association with others who were choosing to make harmful decisions. This principle translates to adults too. Make sure you surround yourself with the right people.

If you and I surround ourselves with negative people we will become negative yet on the flip side, if we surround ourselves with positive and successful people, inevitably that is who we will become. We become like the people we associate with. So choose wisely.

Chapter 5

You and Your Network

"The successful networkers I know, the ones receiving tons of referral and feeling truly happy about themselves, continually put the other person's needs ahead of their own".
- Bob Burg-

To ignore your personal network in your quest to changing your world is like trying to drive a car without wheels.

In today's world the lone ranger is just that - 'alone.' There have been times in human development when the thinking comprised of 'me, myself and I' was deemed to be ok; this kind of outlook is not applicable in these times. So who and what is your network? And what types of networks are there? In answering these questions I implore you to keep an open mind. Prepare to unlearn old and defunct methods and learn new methods that are effective in today's world.

One clear denominator is the statement below which needs to be read and re-read for it to sink deep into the psyche;

The wealthy are into networks, while broke people just look for work!

My simple personal definition of networking is "the coming together of separate individuals and entities for the benefit of the collective." We've all heard the old proverb; "together we stand, divided we fall." There is such a huge advantage in the collective. Of all my favourite thought leaders and speakers the late Jim Rohn stands heads and shoulders above them all when he said simply, *"Each of us needs all of us"*. This is a prolific statement because it highlights the truth about our need for each other.

Nature itself shows evidence of this all the time! I was watching a wildlife documentary the other day and I observed how instinctively wild game protect themselves against ferocious predators like, Lions, Tigers, Crocodiles, Leopards and Cheetahs. They move around in a herd and provide cover for their young and weak by sticking them in the middle of the herd. As long as none of them is isolated, the lions and other predators go hungry or find it difficult to break the herd.

The only time these predators eat, is when an unfortunate wild game finds itself stranded and isolated from the herd, that's the only time it becomes vulnerable. At this point then you see lions and other predators taking advantage of this weak spot by running in for the kill, brandishing knives, forks, ketchup and adjusting the napkins around their necks!

In the human jungle, a man without a network is vulnerable and easy prey for all the predators out there! Easy prey without eyes, ears, or legs to avoid being eaten alive!

As I know that being eaten alive isn't anyone's ambition, let us now identify our networks.

Your Personal Network:

These are those people you have in your phone book on your mobile phone as it is with most people. A few keep a book of numbers. In both cases, there are at least over a hundred names and numbers. These numbers translate into immediate family, friends, friends of friends, and acquaintances.

Business Networks:

We have all attended functions and events where we've been handed business cards, people offering goods and services of all varieties and nature.

Religious Networks:

Most religions congregate in places like, Temples, Mosques, Churches, Synagogues and so forth. Places like that create natural networks that are vital to healthy communities, nations, countries and our entire World.

These networks can be invaluable tools in our quest to change our world. With the right skills and know how you will not believe the change that can happen to your life in the next few years.

Now, your network can be active or dormant. An active network is profitable and a desirable thing while a dormant one isn't.

It's just that simple.

ACTIVATE YOUR NETWORK

All you need to activate your network is a phone, the right motive or good intention and something to offer! Before I show you how to use these simple tools, let me first show you the potential of your personal network.

You've got to know the potential in your network, before you can be motivated to pay the price of activating your network, activating your network is simple but not easy, the price is considerable but worth it. Check out the potential hidden in every network of only 100 people!

If you own a mobile phone, you will have a contact list or phone book; somewhere you store the names and numbers of friends, family and acquaintances.

An average phone book on a mobile phone contains over 100 names; let's assume the average annual income of each person in the UK is £20,000 - that means in every mobile phone, for every 100 names, there is a potential disposable income of £2,000,000 (Two million pounds!) potential disposable income! My question to you, and your question to yourself should be, what percentage of the £2 million comes to you?

That's only for every 100 people; think of how many lots of 100 people are around you at your church, your college, your community, at Mega Churches, Mosques and Synagogues. If this money isn't coming to you, it is going somewhere else! I think we should be interested in finding out where it all goes, shouldn't we? What do we spend our money on? For Food there is Sainsbury's, Tesco, Morrison's and cartel of retailers. For Telecommunication we seek out BT, T-mobile, Orange, O2 and a smorgasbord of providers. For Clothing we choose Next, Gap, Tommy Hilfiger, Polo, think of what you spend your money on, and think of what others you know spend their money on. We all spend our money on goods and services.

Now think of your life, do you make any money from any of these goods and services, if you do, great, you are getting your share of the pie, but if you are not; I believe you should ask yourself why not?

To get your slice of this pie, you will need to develop some basic skills in what I call "Activating your Network." Are you still open minded? Remember the statement we examined at the beginning of this chapter. Go back and re-read it again!

HOW TO ACTIVATE YOUR NETWORK

You will need to develop the skill of calling people on your phone and engaging them with a business idea or service that they need and they are willing to pay for. We all call people and probably talk about many things, the latest film we saw, the latest information making the rounds, what's going on in town, and most importantly what has impacted you.

You already call people, why not direct your energy when you do, to sharing mutually beneficial ideas, finding out what people you know are into or maybe interested in; with the intention of helping them get what they desire?

When I started the journey of activating my network, Simon, remember him? Simon was my coach and I remember him telling me to smile at people every morning and say hello.

At first I thought it was odd smiling at people, but I decided to give it a go, yes there were times when I smiled and said hello to strangers first thing in the morning and I found I had to help them out of the bushes, from fright and shock or both and after dusting them off they would scramble off in such a haste. They must have all been convinced I was either intending to mug them or do some other kind of mischief. I didn't let the reactions I was getting stop me, I chose to keep at it, now I find the payback is amazing!

It took some time but people stopped being startled at my hellos and beaming smile. It then became natural to acquaint myself with people on trains, buses and other public places, some of these acquaintances have today become very good friends; friends that have added to my life in numerous ways. It has now become a very profitable skill to me. I say this because you never know to whom the next person you are extending your hand of friendship to.

Once you get this skill under your belt, meeting new people constantly can be an amazing source of information and upward mobility. I must clarify here that people are not to be seen as inanimate objects to be used by you but in fact, to be treasured for the value they bring to the relationship. People are priceless gifts in the story of living on purpose.

I remember some years ago, as I was keeping up the habit of saying hello to strangers, there was this gentleman I always walked past on my way to work everyday. As we passed each other going in opposite directions, I would nod, smile and if I catch his attention, say hello.

On several occasions of doing this, I observed he wasn't responding or he wouldn't respond. So I decided not to stop, sure enough next day was the same, and the next, it got to a point I got used to him ignoring my hellos; so you can imagine my surprise one day when he said hello back! It took a lot of self control not to jump in surprise. That's how I got to know William, a mild mannered giant with a good heart, we became very good friends. From his perspective it looked odd that a total stranger would go out of his way to say hello to him every morning, then he said I would always add "God bless you", he said that got him intrigued to the point that he said he couldn't help but respond.

The above shows us that reaching out might not always be easy, but with perseverance, you will get the sure reward. In my case I made an acquaintance who later became a friend.

THE POWER OF LISTENING

It is quite hard for an untrained mind to engage in listening. However, listening is a crucial skill to have when engaged in the art of activating networks.

After you have developed the skill of making new acquaintances, you will now need to listen and listen carefully. You see what many years of research has shown me is that everyone has a desire; they have something that makes their heart pound with excitement just at the thought of it. Simply put; we all want something!

My something is 'Freedom!' I prize the freedom very high, the freedom to do what I want, when I want, with whom I want, and for as long as I want. This is freedom to me. That's my hot button; find your own hot button, what you desire so flagrantly in your life. Once you find it you will know; because just the thought of it will bring a twinkle in your eyes and make your heart beat sharply and a host of other sensations will flood your body just at the thought of that one thing you desire. I am not talking here of attraction to the opposite sex, I just thought I'd make that clear as the sensations can be quite similar. I am talking about dreams, goals, aspirations and ambitions that you know draw upon every fibre of your being and it will not release you until you reach the place called 'there'. Having said that there is a chapter in the book 'Think and Grow Rich' on the power of Sexual Transmutation, it is definitely worth a read.

Now everybody has their own hot button as explained in the above paragraphs. When activating your network you have to find out what people's hot buttons are. If you don't, you will quickly become a bore.

The only way to find out what peoples hot buttons are is by listening to them, finding out what interests them, asking questions and keeping quiet. Too often one does find people who are just interested in themselves, interested only in their own interests. They love the sound of their own voice and wouldn't let anyone else contribute to the conversation they are having. This is a definite no-no when trying to activate networks. Patience in this aspect is crucial. I must add it is learned behavior and anyone can acquire it in varying degrees.

As most people are selfish, listening is hard because listening is generous. When one listens, one is being generous. When one doesn't listen the opposite is the case - one is being selfish.

Activating one's network must never be done with a selfish outlook as I alluded to earlier, that is, trying to activate your network so that you can make money by using people, working hard trying to outsmart people; it never works. It might work temporarily but in the long run, people would eventually figure out what's going on and back away from you like you have a bad stink on you.

GENEROSITY

Generosity is the key to activating any network. Yes, there is profit in activating our networks, but the route to it is generosity. By listening to people with a pure motive of getting to know what's interesting about them, what's unique about them and what you can do to support them on their journey; only a generous person can walk that road. To add value to each other one or both parties must have a clear understanding that generosity demands a preferring of the other so that success can be shared.

In my opinion the most important component for success in life and business is 'People'. People buy stuff, invent stuff, distribute stuff, and subscribe to stuff. It is people that follow stuff, endorse stuff, and testify on behalf of stuff. Take people out of the equation, all you are left with is stuff, and without people wanting and liking stuff, stuff very quickly becomes junk! And that's the life-changing truth the world misses every time.

If you are not a generous person, and you are not willing to learn to develop a heart of generosity, you will have to ignore this chapter; this chapter is not for you. Ignoring this warning will do more harm to yourself and your reputation. If you proceed with your old selfish motives, you will find the attempt to work with people not only frustrating but unfruitful. Selfish people don't make good leaders, the only other way open for them is to pay cash for loyalty, and demand loyalty because they are paying for it. Now without stating it mildly that is the ugly picture which when examined closely, you can put all the despots, dictators and the vilest people on the planet in this frame.

Sort of what is happening in most work and living environments nowadays!

ENGAGING YOUR NETWORK

Apparently with these new skills; the choice to be friendly and saying hello, making new acquaintances constantly, listening to people and finding out what their hot button is, having the right 'Motive', cultivating a 'History' (Track record) and sharing the 'Example' will now qualify you for engaging your network successfully. I guarantee the with these tools you will now be in a position to stake a claim to part of the £2 million a year for every 100 people you know and meet.

THE NEED FOR A MENTOR

A mentor is an invaluable agent to our quest of activating our networks. I have had and continue to have many mentors that have helped and continue to help shape my life. A mentor in my book is somebody, anybody who is willing to help someone else get to their desired destination.

A mentor could be a peer or a person who has already achieved the things you now going after. You can have a mentor for every aspect of your life.

Mentoring requires a lot of commitment, sacrifice and self denial, to genuinely help someone walk from ignorance to enlightenment – from darkness to light.

A mentor says: "let me save you time and effort by showing you a quicker, better, more profitable way. I have been there, done that and this is what I have found are the things I would do different now with the advantage of hind sight. You don't have to make the mistakes that I have made. Come let me show you all the secrets." That is what a true mentor should be able to say and do. A mentor is like a coach. A coach brings out the best potential out any athlete who cares about his/her progress.

My first mentor in the UK was Laurence Dyer, even though I didn't think he was mentoring me, I look back now and realize that was exactly what he was doing. What started out as a casual friendship, turned out to be a catalyst for a life changing journey for me. Laurence taught me a lot of things. Laurence taught me how to play chess, monopoly, Risk (A game of military strategy). Being taught these games were a huge impact on my life because of my peculiar learning style. I am like a sponge when I find something I'm interested in, and I am interested in 'Life' so teaching me strategic games like chess, monopoly, Risk was teaching me things about life that I hadn't learnt before.

Every time I played chess, it exercised my tactical and analytical muscles. I saw government policy and the impact it had on the common man, in chess the King and Queen and the other officials were the ruling class and they made moves all intended to protect the King. The pawn - the common man was very expendable, however a pawn although expendable and had the least power could be used to check mate a King.

I started seeing how tactically I could raise my station in life regardless of what card fate had supposedly dealt me.

When Laurence taught me how to play monopoly, he taught me well, and little did he know that it was through monopoly that he was teaching me how money flowed in society, how to use little properties effectively to rule those with big properties and most especially the art of making deals. Monopoly is won and lost on your ability to negotiate good deals. Today some people tell me that one of my strongest ability in business is making mutually beneficial deals.

It all came from Laurence teaching me how to play monopoly. Mentoring is a crown to the head that will humbly wear it.

Whenever I played Risk with Laurence I started understanding how armies could be deployed around the world, how military success is not just a matter of bigger numbers, and how geographical locations of continents can be used strategically.

I believe in my case, apart from learning how to read and write, I will trade my entire primary and secondary school education for what Laurence taught me any day! Bang goes the theory that 'education' can only be achieved with four walls of academia.

MY NETWORK ACTIVATION MENTOR

Not very long after learning such great stuff from Laurence, I met Simon Ginns. Simon became my mentor for many years. Isn't it just like God to make me grow up in Africa but never really engaged my destiny until I met these two white brothers; my brothers from another mother coining the American phrase..

Simon would invite me to Amway meetings in places like Ipswich, Harrogate, Leeds, Birmingham and Scotland, he would arrange to pick me up at a station near me, because in those days I didn't drive. He would pick me up and drive for many, many miles. We would attend functions at some of the most picturesque locations in Britain and afterwards he would drop me back home in East London about 1am in the morning and still have another hour's drive to get back to his house.

He did this selflessly for many years, I don't know if he knew what he was doing then, but he left an indelible impression on this life of mine. Simon was so generous that he would treat me like an equal. Simon a young bachelor in those days and in his early thirties, had a big 2 bedroom house, drove the latest models of Mercedes Benz and was I believe, a sales director with BT. This guy seemed to have it all, but he treated me who had nothing, relatively fresh from Nigeria; as an equal. I never felt inferior around Simon, I felt like a contemporary. Simon made me feel like I belonged and I would undoubtedly very soon have all the trappings he had and more.

He would treat me as an equal again in that he would never pay my way. If a ticket had to be bought for my use, he would give me the privilege of paying for it. It was a privilege because he made sure I took responsibility for what I could, for example whenever we went to a McDonalds' Simon would never attempt to pay for my order; he paid for he's and I always paid for mine.

Simon's relationship with me wasn't to give me a fish, he's was to teach me how to fish, so I can have fish anytime I wanted for the rest of my life. If the 'First World' treated the 'Third World' like this, there will be no more 'Third World'.

I haven't seen Simon for many years now, but now I have all the fish I want, because I now know how to fish. Thanks to Simon I don't need him anymore, all I need him for now is to be present when I say thank you. Thank you on my behalf and on behalf of all the people whose life has been touched, and continue to be touched and will be touched all because one man mentored another.

A mentor's role if done right; is always to mentor till the student doesn't need them anymore. In other words they teach themselves out of the job. It is a selfless but extremely rewarding path that only the great can walk. One day a student must become a master or the work is not yet done. It is an act of raising someone from the dust with an intention of that person surpassing where you are one day. A mentor is a balcony person; he/she will cheer you on in the race.

If you ask me; that is what I call a true Mentor.

WHERE CAN ONE FIND MENTORS?

I have been fortunate to have experienced one on one mentoring, obviously reflected in the stories I have written about Laurence and Simon. However, I have also found that one can be mentored through other means, reading books is one; I have found some classic books that mentored me in specific areas of my life. Books like "How to win friends and influence people" continue to mentor me on how to build successful relationships with people. So books can also be effective mentors because the mind of the author is still revealing the things you need to go to the next level. A person who will not read or become hungry for knowledge is in great danger of being a fool whose end is predictably known.

AT PROJX INTERNATIONAL

You will find more about ProjX International at the closing chapters of this book. It is worth a good mention because mentors are being mentored to mentor at ProjX International.

While mentors are very much needed in our world today, the sad truth is that there are very few I would say are mentoring material. Most fall into the trap of just becoming bosses, or worse still take advantage of people by abusing the privilege afforded to them. What's the difference between a boss and a mentor? Simple; a boss manages people into action, while a mentor inspires people into action.

One is leadership by force, "do as I say or else!" While the other is leadership by consent, "do as I do!"

Be discerning when you hear the word leadership. This powerful principle has been abused by many so much that it means next to nothing.

Review your understanding of leadership and pay extreme attention to any re-definition of it. The principles remain the same whilst the methods continue to change.

A WORD OF CAUTION

You must choose wisely when considering who would mentor you. It must be someone or a philosophy that you can vouch for explicitly. For example your financial mentor must be sound financially; your moral mentor must be without question the best in your opinion morally, so on and so forth. I wanted to be my own boss, so I chose mentors that were not only their own bosses but very successful at it.

There were many people on the other hand who proposed to mentor me in my quest to be financially free and independent, but they were stuck in dead end jobs and were in the classic 40 year rut plan, as eloquent as they were I wisely said - “thanks but no thanks.” I learnt very early on in my journey that opinions are very cheap, anyone can offer one; what’s more important is the active commitment that follows any opinion offered. If anyone offers me any opinion and I see there is no commitment backing it up, it is as worthless as the dust that gathers on the sole of my shoes. To make this point even clearer, how many people do you think have an opinion on how Arsene

Wenger can make Arsenal a better team? Answer: Everyone! But only Arsene Wenger is fully committed because he is the one that has a job to lose if things don't work out well at Arsenal. You and I, unless we apply for the managerial job and are successful at it are just bumping gums! "Opinions as they say are cheap."

MY LAST WORD ON MENTORING

Once you have found yourself a good mentor, you must remember that your quest is not to be a clone of your mentor. Your mentor must only be a guide to you discovering yourself. You must develop what's unique about you as that is where your greatness lies. God could have created us all uniform but he didn't. He created us with unique qualities; even identical twins have got a galaxy of differences when closely examined.

Remember a time will come when the student becomes a master. Learning as we know is a life-long endeavour and not an event.

At some point we must achieve a stage where we have developed our own original ideas, our own personal convictions and outlook. Yes they might be coloured by the ideas of our former mentors but only coloured, not the sum total of our entire philosophy or belief-system.

We must always at the final analysis let our actions be a result of our own personal convictions.

Interlude

A Tribute to Network Marketing

NETWORK MARKETING: THE UGLY DUCKLING OF THE MARKETING WORLD

Network marketing is almost always a misunderstood phenomenon. Most people, don't like it, don't want it, can't stand it, have tried it and it's left a bad taste, a bad smell, and some people are just downright scared of it.

I love Network Marketing. It is the network marketing environment that groomed me because it gave me the exposure nobody from my background was able to give me. It suited my learning style so well. It taught me leadership by example, taught me how to dream and reach for those dreams… I could go on and on… I owe even my ability to write this book to my exposure to Network Marketing. Many people that have tried it and have had a bad experience usually have been victims of people who were not properly skilled in the art of Network marketing or worst still the people who don't have the heart for Network Marketing.

THE BAD PRESS!!! VICTIM: NETWORK MARKETING

A plethora of people unfortunately label Network Marketing "Pyramid!" It is an unfortunate mistake that precludes them from enjoying the amazing benefits that exist in Network Marketing.

The difference is what people term "Pyramid" is a scam! This is a scam that is driven primarily by greed and a chronic lack of trust.

Two Types of 'the' Scam

They are easy to spot as they usually don't have any goods or services attached to their schemes. Alarm bells should start going off in your head, whenever anyone says to you "Introduce two people into our system, invest £7000, and as soon as you do that, we'll pay you £21,000." Please always ask them, what goods are we selling? What service are we offering? If the answer is nothing! Run as far as you can and as fast as you can! (All they are doing is paying old investors with new investor's money!). As we all know robbing Peter to pay Paul only leads to Peter chasing you for what he's owed; and that is why these schemes always end in disaster.

The other is a bit more sophisticated, as they in fact, do have goods or services. The scam is usually run on a wholesaler level. A lot of stock is worth £10,000, Mr. A buys it for £12,000, Mrs. B buys the same lot for £14,000, and gullible Mr. C buys the same lot off Mrs. B for £16,000 by the time this same stock passes through more hands, the stock is so expensive. (It becomes priced above the market). In other words it's all a game of passing the buck, until someone is left holding the buck and a whole heap of debt!

Network Marketing is worlds away from the two illustrations stated above. Network Marketing not only has goods and services; there is no mark up on the price within its membership.

This means everyone within the network gets the product or service at the same price! (No passing the buck!) Compensation is then allocated directly proportional to the size of one's team within the Network.

UNVIELING THE SWAN

Network Marketing to me is simply marketing through a network; be it a personal or a professional network. Seeing it any other way as far as I am concerned is complicating the otherwise simple. Studies have shown since the beginning of time that word of mouth is the most powerful form of advertising available to man – it is available to any man; hence in a world where advertising through other means usually costs a packet; Network Marketing in my view is here to stay and not only stay but thrive to levels not yet seen by the world at large.

THE BENEFITS ARE TREMENDOUS!

One of the greatest benefits for me has been personal development, closely followed by the unbelievable quality of relationships that naturally develops in a Network Marketing environment.

The cash flow, the overrides, the passive incomes, the comradeship, the healthy competition, the cheerleading, the pats on the back, the high fives, the sometimes embarrassingly crazy party atmospheres at functions, are all things that set Network Marketing apart in the sales industry. It was the first environment I saw where people dared to dream, and dared to dream big. The first environment where I witnessed people commit themselves to a goal, and hold themselves accountable to a collective, and manage to do it all in a healthy way.

Network Marketing has a way of purging its ranks of shady characters, which allows only the very best to succeed. Authentic Network Marketing is best at believing in people, is most excellent at having other people's best interest at heart, unsurpassed at genuinely serving, best at caring, is finest at leading by example. Show me someone successful, really successful in Network Marketing and I'll show you a real winner! This is a person who has worked tremendously hard on him or herself. I will show you a winner that wins on several levels and an individual that is skilled to a level that nearly defies belief.

It's an environment that demands people to work on themselves, an environment where people can't hide, so only serious people need apply.

Network Marketing is an environment where you are encouraged to take on winning habits; habits like reading, setting and meeting goals, being accountable, facing your fears, getting used to the uncomfortable, and the inconvenient. Success is never achieved on the road of comfort and convenience.

I was exposed to winner's mantras like 'If it is to be, it's up to me', 'Winners never quit and quitters never win!', 'No excuses will be accepted; so none should be given!', 'Do it now!' and so many more.

I am fiercely proud to spend the rest of my time on this planet, with people that are willing to subject themselves to the refining fire of paying the price of being the very best they can be.

I must confess that I find a lot of these kinds of people in Network Marketing.

HOW DARE I?

Dare I say that Network Marketing could be the answer to a lot of the ills in the world today?

When I got to this country in 1990 it didn't take long to understand that my lovely dark skin wasn't appreciated by everyone. I experienced it on the tube, on the streets, at work, practically everywhere but in Network Marketing.

I quickly realized that my up-line didn't care if I was black, white, or Chinese; all they saw was a kindred spirit, someone on their team who dared to dream. They shared everything with me, they withheld nothing, I mean nothing, none of this "let's keep him from knowing this or that" which was the sentiment of my colleagues at work; because you see in Network Marketing, my success meant their success too! So if they slowed me down they invariably slowed themselves down. Truth be said, we all have these preferences and prejudices. In Network Marketing everyone quickly learns to discard all these backward baggage.

It was in a networking environment that I experienced holding hands with two other men, charged with the overwhelming power of the moment, one is a Sikh with his hair wrapped in his turban, the other a Caucasian of German origin and me an African, and in that moment, we might as well have come from the same womb. They were both my brothers as any biological brother could ever be! Quite a prolific scenario of reality change that crosses so many barriers, wouldn't you agree?

ALL THE WORLD'S ILL…

In retrospect, I discovered that the ills that have plagued this world of ours expire as the diseases they are; in the antiseptic environment of Network Marketing.

Sexism, ageism, racism, religious fanaticism, negative nationalism and all other forms of 'isms' melt off people under the glaring sun of togetherness found in Network Marketing.

When people are recruiting people for their Network Marketing business, and I have noticed; they couldn't care less if you were fat, tall, short, thin, ugly, or what your status is, it is amazing! All they see is what's inside. Tell me where else do you find that?

FIX UP OR GET OUT!

As with everything in life, there are those within the industry that are giving the whole industry a bad name. This is my advice: fix up or get out! The interesting thing is that the industry naturally weeds out the bad eggs, they usually don't last. For all of you out there that fell into the hands of these undesirables, take comfort from the fact that they self destruct without fail and quite quickly.

To those who are building their networks the right way, and are working hard to build long lasting businesses and relationships, please keep going, because the world needs you now more than ever! I raise my imaginary or metaphoric champagne glass to you all and say… "Here is to the future!"

My Prediction

I stated earlier that Network Marketing was the ugly duckling of the marketing industry, and just like the fairy tale, I believe Network Marketing will develop from an ugly ducking into a beautiful Swan.

The world is changing fast, so fast that the changes are not leaving enough time for people to adjust, the only time people know about the change is when it hits them, and it hits them hard, sometimes too hard. They know about the change when yet another redundancy hits them, under the age of 35 they've been made redundant 3 times already! It hits them when their career or profession, something they have been doing for over 30yrs asks them to retrain to keep their job. When they started the job everything was paper based, they got good at that in fact they got so good at that, I'm thinking about the medical profession here, My mother after over 35years of being a nurse, first started noticing that her bosses weren't even born when she was a Matron Surgical nurse, she tried to put up with that then bang! In her 60s she was asked to retrain, learn to use computers, for diagnosis, administration etc. I couldn't help but notice her pain when it dawned on her that the Fat lady had sung! It was now all over.

I saw her even try to go to the computer classes, only to come back home to tell me that she slept at the console, I even tried to teach her a thing or two but I noticed her heart wasn't in it. So my mother took the only option left, she retired.

Some of us can remember when being a Secretary was a respectable career. I remember some mates of mine studying typing as a subject. Oh how things have changed so fast that Secretaries have morphed into Personal Assistants and P.As are now morphing into organizers on personal computers and smart phones. Every career path is undergoing this inevitable change, Banking, Architecture, Accounting, Law, every career path is taking this hit, and as they take the hit people are being displaced, which means more job losses, more redundancies, more pressures on families, relationships, communities and nations.

In this kind of business environment, companies are going to be less inclined to offer what they used to. In times past companies would give you a job with packages like sick pay, bonuses, and retirement plans. Well they don't have to do that anymore, not long ago the government started encouraging people to go for company pensions, they would support the companies they said. Now companies are nudging people into having private pensions. The writing is on the wall folks! Nobody is going to take care of anybody in the long run; we'd all have to take care of ourselves, period!

Traditional businesses depended on 'Capital' they got from banks, with collateral and monthly repayments. This form of business financing has taken a huge hit because of the default avalanche the world experienced lately. Even banks defaulted on their loans; talk less of companies and ordinary businessmen or homeowners. The whole market came crashing and the word 'Credit Crunch' was born and etched into all our psyches.

More and more companies will go the Network Marketing way!

Credit crunch or not, people still need goods and services. People still need to take their bath, brush their teeth use health products, use utilities like gas, electricity, broadband internet, cable TV, insurance, and mortgages. As you can see the list can go on and on, now the option these companies have is to spend millions and hundreds of millions on advertising and compete with the most powerful form of advertising – word of mouth. My prediction is they will choose more and more to market their offering through Network Marketing vehicles which is based primarily on word of mouth.

Why? Because it is ultimately far more cost effective, the customer base can be far more fiercely loyal, and people have far more opportunity to buy into the company; so the overall responsibility of the company's success can be share with eager and willing stake holders. This leads to even more company profits and business targets being achieved with less strain on the overall company budget.

It's a no brainer!

My prediction is that Network Marketing that used to attract sneers and jeers, which people used to spit at and reject outright, that people use to unfairly label 'pyramid' would be for most people in the coming years, one of the only few remaining avenues for earning income, achieving upward mobility, and realizing the dreams that we all yearn for. Oh yes the traditional way of doing business will remain, but I predict Network Marketing will be the new 'in thing' the world over.

More and more people will go the Network Marketing way.

As careers continue to take the hit they've been taking for years, and as people continue to be displaced from the market place, through redundancies, automation or less demand for a workforce, more people and more people will slowly realize that Network Marketing is the way to go. I appreciate that this will scare the living day light out of a lot of folk, but hey change is inevitable. Apparently when the first cars were unleashed on the streets, it scared the living day lights out of people that have only ever seen horses. There was an apparent outcry, so for a while the authorities came up with a compromise, and the compromise was that cars would only be allowed on the streets if they had a man walking in front of the car waving a flag and shouting, "Horseless carriage approaching – beware!"

How absurd right?

Rather than being afraid of it, my suggestion is to study, understand and embrace change.

Most people will say "but I don't like selling!" Well, in today's world that's just like an illiterate at the turn of the century saying "but I don't like reading and writing!"

"Well tough!" Is the sentiment of the market place. "Stay broke!" remain at the bottom of the ladder, and as we all know, the problem with being at the bottom of the ladder is there are too many backsides above you, backsides that have natural tendencies to let go of foul air and dung!

No! What you want to do is pay the price of breathing fresh air; fresh air is always at the top never at the bottom.

The price put in black and white is learning and embracing new skills like, writing a list, calling people on your list, and sharing your opportunity with them. Now that in my book is not too much a price to pay! Yes you might have to venture out of your comfort zone, but no one is saying you should storm a building suspected to be filled with Terrorists and booby traps. In other words you won't be blown into pieces, lose your life or a limb. On the contrary you have everything to gain, higher self esteem, better self image, a sense of accomplishment, and if you really pay the price in full and in advance, the life of your dreams.

The Pioneer's reward:

You be the pioneer, you be one of the select few that'll run and grab the land like they did in the early days of the United States of America; 1889 to be precise, it was called the Land Run of 1889, where people had to run and stake a claim to unassigned land. Imagine running and staking a claim to untold acres of land?

It's called instant wealth! The pioneer's reward!

What I have been trying to say all this while is that there is a new frontier, a new frontier in the world of commerce and business, it's called Network Marketing.

Just like it is ludicrous to try and go to the US now for a Land Run, so will it be in a few years to start running and staking your claim in the Network Marketing world.

The time to run is now! Most people will unfortunately make the mistake of running when everyone accepts that Network Marketing is the way to go. By that time my friends it will be too late.

You start believing before everyone else, you start running before everyone else, you start building and investing before everyone else, that is the only way you will qualify for the pioneer's reward that will be shared in this brave new frontier.

To your success!

Mr. Phil

Chapter 6

The Great Divide

"The great dividing line between success and failure can be expressed in five words: "I do not have the time".
- Anonymous -

We live in a time where "really living" is hard to achieve and just existing is what most people manage to accomplish. People without jobs look forward to getting one so they can move away from being broke all the time. I call this living in 'broke-Ville', at the same time those that have jobs find themselves not only still broke, but increasingly sick and tired of being sick and tired. What a combination to have to endure on a daily basis! It beggars belief that many are ready to resign themselves to this kind of life when they have in their hands the tools to fashion their world!

While we can't say that this is the hardest time to live in, other generations before ours will rightfully challenge us by reminding us of the fact that they lived without a lot of things we take for granted today. Imagine the gadgets and infrastructures designed with one express aim of making our lives easier. Smart mobile phones, internet with high speed broadband connections, HD appliances, TVs the size of satellite dishes not to mention the dishes themselves. There are hand held camcorders, and a new generation of electronic equipments that aim to create real life experiences in our homes like cinema quality pictures and sounds that are threatening to make going to the Cinema itself obsolete. Then there are cars that seem not only to have a mind of their own but are almost willing to drive themselves.

We are surrounded by the most beautiful things and have more toys than any other time in human history, yet we are more dissatisfied with our lives than the previous generations. Most of us just exist day to day, week to week, month to month until the years pile up and there seems to be no let up on the feeling of personal and collective hopelessness.

How many people can really say they love the life they are living? How many can say categorically that they absolutely love what they do and are not settling for less? While I am not saying there aren't such people, what I am saying is that they are definitely few and far between. The norm is that a majority of people are just trying to sustain their existence by paying for this bill and that bill, never getting a chance to really do what their heart desires and what their heart cries out desperately for. In a manner of speaking they are trying hard as they may to make ends meet; only to discover that the ends keep moving.

The divide between our daily lives and the life our heart desires is what I call 'the great divide'. In a world where celebrity has become the epitome of the good life, at least that is what the media alludes to. This is despite the fact that we see their broken and shattered lives, be it divorces, strings of illicit affairs, continuous brushes with the law and even a mounting rate of suicide among these people; and these are the people that are portrayed as having it all! It really makes one scratch one's head and wonder, what is this so called good life? Is it the Holy Grail of our modern world? This is where the thinking mind makes the distinction.

There is such desperation in the air to "make it", that one can almost see people froth at the mouth at the prospects of 'making it'. While it isn't wrong to be ambitious, in my opinion being desperate and willing to do anything just to make it has got to be so wrong for obvious reasons.

This desperation is so bad now that you need only watch TV after 8pm (why the watershed?), and a deluge of undressed frolicking men and women who spew immorality and foul language is all that is available to watch. It is apparent that money laced with decadent greed has got to be the only motivation for anyone in their right mind, to agree to the kinds of degradation we see on our TV screens much less on the silver screens.

Just imagine the young innocent girls and boys lured into the dark seedy underground world of all kinds of vice, and ask yourself what would make an innocent boy or girl go down that path? I believe it is the constant barrage of images that proclaim subliminally - "greed is good", "without money you are nothing", "look after number one"... "Go get yours!" these messages are responsible for the collective moral decay of our societies today.

Next time you watch the new generation of TV programming; Reality TV shows like American idol, X factor, The Apprentice, Making the Band and the plethora of the other "you-got-to-make-it –or-else" shows that litter our screens. As you watch you note the palpable desperation the contestant has to "make it", it is glaring to the discerning eye to see the highs of those who win and the lows of those that believe they have just lost their one and only chance to "make it".

The readiness to stab each other in the back and to trample on the weak is the common sight our dog eat dog world accepts and calls it entertainment. Week after week we watch virtual dreams crushed or kept alive by the voting audience, while the machinery of greed rips off the uninformed who are titillated to numbness.

There was a time in human history when human beings were still apparently on the road to being civilized. One classic example of this was ancient Rome where experienced and so-called civilized people watched other people being slaughtered in the name of entertainment. In the Coliseum gladiators declared before they engaged their opponents with these words "We who are about to die salute you."

Pundits had their favourite gladiator and they even voted with their thumbs up or thumb down, which should live or die… an uncanny similarity to what we are being fed on TV nowadays with reality shows isn't it? We must ask ourselves why the people of Rome indulged in such a barbaric spectacle. Well at that time, the Emperor staged this gladiatorial combats so that the populace would be anesthetized from the pain of their daily lives. While you have just been to a place where another human being's body has been decapitated or torn limb from limb, it has a way of impressing on you the need to realize you are at least better off than someone else, while at the same time eroding your sense of outrage and dulling your sense of reasoning.

DON'T FALL FOR THE CON

If you want to change your world, you cannot afford to buy into the 'desperation culture'. Very frequently in the business hob of the City of London – young men and women commit suicide by leaping off tall buildings, leap in front of trains or other insensitive means. Have you ever wondered why a stock broker, supposedly successful in a particular environment where they receive millions personally in bonuses; why then would they suddenly decide they've grown wings and it's time to go for a test flight?

I think about it, and in my opinion, I believe when people are too eager and too desperate to succeed they preclude themselves always and without fail, from having a chance of getting what they so desperately desire! Nick Leeson the trader that brought down Barings Bank bought into this culture and paid with time in jail and the reputation of being - The Rouge trader! In my opinion he got stuck in the status game.

BEWARE OF THE STATUS GAME

If anyone knows about status, I believe it's got to be a guy like me; and my credentials? Growing up in Nigeria! That is all anyone needs to be a PHD in understanding status.

I do realize that status is everywhere and in every culture; however we Africans take it to another level. I remember my first hand me down designer shirt, it wasn't even brand new but it was 'designer', I was over the moon, because this now gave me the right to look down on some people as they don't have a 'designer' shirt.

I wonder where I got that kind of warped thinking from. Could it have been assimilated by living in a culture where the rich drive around in exotic air conditioned vehicles in a country where the roads are riddled with pot holes the size of craters? Did I learn it by watching the poor doomed to poverty by the misfortune of being born into a poor family?

Could it be that growing up in an environment where I saw the so called rich oppressing the under-privileged that sowed the seed of status in me? In secondary school, I can remember the status inducing effects in electing subjects that promised the prospects of becoming a Doctor, Lawyer, Engineer or an Architect. Those who learned typing or commercial subjects were looked down on and considered to be dunces or second rate humans. Parents would boast with words like 'my son is in medical school', my daughter is studying to become an Engineer' and they would not associate with another parent whose child was studying carpentry. Now to think of it, how absurd it was for us children who in fact, had other ideas about what we desired to do.

It's all a crying shame, as people are willing to be so shallow as to tie their self esteem and self worth to a profession or to the kind of house they live in and the car they drive. It's a travesty that we live in a world where people's identities are so immersed in their profession that they don't even know who they are without the label or badge of their status.

The truth is nobody has to right to look down on anybody; regardless of what they have or don't have. The house a man lives in or the car a man drives cannot be the sole determinant of a man or woman's worth. The moment I look down on any of God's creation, I have just instantly given someone else the right to look down on me. That in itself is a futile game. Our self worth and self esteem have got to be divorced from what we have been able to accumulate or not acquired as the case may be.

Someone might ask what about people in authority? Presidents, Prime Ministers, or even the

Queen, my simple answer is yes they have authority by virtue of their responsibilities, however they cannot claim to be better than you or I until they can truly prove they have control of every breath they take! God created all men equal as he holds every man's breath without which no one can do anything.

The downside of this game is; once you tie your self esteem and self worth to a Ferrari, what happens when it is gone? If I have learnt anything in this game of life, it is that nothing is permanent, life goes up and down, a villain today could be the hero of tomorrow, ask Nelson Mandela. The hero today could be the villain tomorrow. Think of Adolph Hitler and the German people… A superpower today could be wiped off the map and the pages of history, ask the people of Carthage a superpower civilization that rivaled Rome. Everything is transient but God.

If there is any lesson that history has taught from the dawn of time, it is that things come and go. An individual with money today can lose everything tomorrow and someone famed today can suddenly be reduced to a has-been tomorrow. The person basking in the trappings of success today; best cars, palatial homes, private jet and money in billions can lose it all. I know it beggars belief that it can happen – but it certainly does. Have you not seen it yourself?

"When one is defined by what they own, then what they own ends up owning them!"–Mr. Phil

One's self worth and self esteem has got to be divorced from what they own, and what other people think of them. This way when the ups and downs of life happen, they can carry on living a healthy life. If one's life is tied to status and what other people think about them or will think about them, when things go wrong, as they do, they find themselves not able to bear the fall from the virtual grace; virtual because it was never real, and other people's opinion that creates this form of grace that they supposedly fall from is vastly over-rated. That is too much power to give anyone or any set of people.

BUDDHIST MONKS

I have read stories of superstar actors and musicians leaving all the hype, all the glamour, all the lifestyle and fame. They are leaving all these behind to spend supposedly, quality time with Buddhist monks on the picturesque mountains of the Himalayas.

Buddhist monks adhere to a strict code of austere living by denying themselves any sort of pleasure. By choice they own nothing and want to own nothing, whilst they devote their lives to meditation and achieving what they call a Zen like state.

What is amazing is that these superstars look up to these monks; they call them their guru meaning master. Now think about it, what would make a superstar actor with all the fame and money call a Buddhist monk with nothing in this world to his name, I mean literarily nothing but the robe on his back – Master! This should make us all think hmmm… isn't that interesting! Could it be that these monks are so content and so reconciled with themselves, that these celebrities coming from the world of designer labels and red carpet fame actually envy and respect these monks and desire to achieve that level of self realization? While we can't all become Buddhist monks or superstars I believe we can learn that our value or worth does not have to come from what we own or how others perceive us.

There are very few people that have the privileged of doing what they love and love what they do.

THE 'FORTUNATE ONES'

I believe everyone should strive to do what they love, and make a living doing it and loving what they do! From personal observation people that love what they do fall into two categories; the first are the 'Fortunate ones' and the second category are the 'Go getters'... The fortunate ones are those people that happen to find they have a natural love for what they do and discover themselves making a living from it.

Some sports personalities fall into this category, footballers like Ronaldinho fall into this category.

Observe him in a football game and it is obvious this is someone who would play even if he doesn't get paid as his enjoyment of the game is apparent.

Some people have talent in a particular area; however this doesn't guarantee they would enjoy a profession that employs their talent. Staying with football, I was watching a documentary on retired footballers; and Gary Leniker although one of the most prolific strikers in English football history said he didn't really enjoy playing football, that to him it was job and no more. Apparently he'd rather be presenting TV shows.

Loving and enjoying what you do that pays the bills is very rare, in some instances it is even frowned upon as people would feel it is unfair; while most people make a living hard grafting so to speak and some just seem to work for a few months and earn millions as is the case with successful individuals in many industries.

THE 'GO GETTERS'

Let's consider the 'go-getters' lifestyles before becoming famous. They would probably be written off as lazy people, as they would lie in and seem to loaf about while they hone their skills. These persons would probably have the landlord or landladies on their backs, as they would be broke all the time, friends and family would be advising them to go and get a regular job as their bills mount up with no remedy in sight.

Finally, when they land a big acting job and start earning the big bucks, suddenly all the advise of getting a regular job become ridiculous and obsolete as they are now earning a sizeable income, and can afford what most people cannot in their entire lifetimes. They now become celebrities and everyone now wishes they had their life, quickly forgetting the years of toil and poverty they had gone through as a price for living the life of their dreams.

THERE IS ALWAYS A PRICE

Society has apparently conditioned us so much that we just accept what we get and not demand what we desire!

There is a conditioning exercise used to tame and train elephants. Apparently if trainers want to train an elephant calf to stay in a particular area and not move about everywhere, what they do is chain it to a particular location with a metal chain, every time it tries to move off the metal chain will prevent it from doing so. After many years of this it finally gets conditioned.

After it is conditioned you can apparently control a huge 20 ton elephant by tying a piece of cotton around it legs and it would not move off because it believes it is prevented by the cotton rope around its legs.

If you ask most people this question: why do you work? They look at you funny, and when they realize you are serious you can literally hear the gears in their brain start working. They've never asked themselves the question! And if you persist in asking, again you will hear the clonk, click, and creek, emanating from the gears of their brains from lack of use. Finally, as if by magic the cliché rolls' "I've got bills to pay" they answer, - yes, so does everybody but not everybody in this world has to survive on a pay packet from a job. Think about it there are many, many ways to make money to pay bills, even things you can do that someone else can elect to pay your bills forever in return for something you've got to offer. We are only limited by how much we use our minds.

Why not live the life you really desire? Why not decide to pay the price? It isn't going to be easy, but the interesting thing I have found about life is that settling for less isn't any easier either. It is just as difficult to stay broke and settle for less as it is to go for the best and demand no less. This is life, isn't it interesting? The truth is that whatever you decide is best for you, inevitably there will be a price to pay.
A Poem from Think and Grow Rich:

"I bargained with Life for a penny,
And life would pay no more,
However I begged at evening
When I counted my scanty store.
"For Life is a just employer,
He gives you what you ask,
But once you have set the wages,
Why, you must bear the task.
"I worked for a Menial's hire,
Only to learn dismayed,
That any wage I had asked of Life,
Life would have willingly paid!"

So why not give yourself, if you haven't already; give yourself the permission to go for what your heart desires, deciding to pay whatever price life demands you pay. It takes guts and determination mixed with unshakable focus, and when you manage to do that, you watch your world change. Remember the title of this book is 'You can change your world', so why not begin your journey now?

Write down what you want out of your life. Be specific about what you want your life to be. Do not worry about what others may think or want for you or from you.

In the final analysis it's what you desire that is important as they can't really see what shines brightly in your heart, only you can feel the beating of the dream that courses within you.

THE WAY PEOPLE SEE YOU

People see you as *they* are not as you are…

If I received a pound for every time someone tells me I can't do this or I can't do that, I would be super wealthy by now. An example may suffice to explain this concept; When a person decides he/she wants to do something, he /she tells people about it and without fail, he/she would be told it won't work. Then it would escalate into a plea not do it, and that he/she will be wasting their time, and on and on it goes in the swaying of the idea he/she had initially. And this is coming from well meaning people, people one may even look up to and because of this one could find it very hard to ignore their advice.

When I want to do something, my experience has taught me to just go ahead and do it, because every time I go ahead and do it, it not only works, not only does it become a blessing, but these same people that said it wasn't a good idea, that it won't work, suddenly develop amnesia and start praising the genius of doing what I had achieved.

It took me a long time, but I think I have finally figured it out! People don't really see you as you are! They see you as they are. What do I mean? You see I finally realized that when I say I want to start a business, or a programme or a project, I would have thought about it and would have worked it all out in my mind; at least I would have worked out a great deal in my mind. When I now tell people, they don't have access to my mind and thinking pattern, what they have access to is their mind and their thinking pattern.

So when I say for instance, I want to run a seminar, I know I am ok with public speaking, they might not be. I know what topics to cover, they don't, I know which venue and how to get people there, they wouldn't even know where to start and to top it all off; I have run seminars before with great success, they haven't and are actually petrified of the prospect.

So you can imagine when I say I want to run a seminar, all they have access to is really their own mind and resources. Once they hear the word 'Seminar' they remember they don't like public speaking, they can't see how they would get people to attend, and they can see the whole idea as a non starter because they can't imagine what topics would engage people and so on.

Anyway, I go ahead and run the seminar, it is well attended and everyone has a really good time, with new contacts made and people are requesting for dates of other seminars I might want to run. Just then I see

Mr. Skeptic walk up to me beaming from ear to ear having just had an amazing time at the seminar, he gives me a bear hug and says, "that was great!

I knew you would do it", as he walks away I am scratching my head thinking – isn't this the same person that said it wouldn't work?

Now I have figured it out. He saw what I proposed through he's own abilities experience and make up. Of course, it wouldn't work for him! But it will work for me because my skills, experience, talents and abilities are altogether different from he's or hers, as skeptics are of all gender, shapes and sizes.

MOST PEOPLE CONTINUALLY MAKE THE MISTAKE OF JUDGING YOU BY THEIR OWN STANDARDS, NOT BY YOUR OWN. INDEED THEY CANNOT JUDGE YOU BY YOUR STANDARD AS THEY DON'T HAVE ACCESS TO YOUR MIND, OR THE RICHES AND RESOURCES YOUR CREATOR HAS PLACED WITHIN YOU.

All they can do is wait on you to express what you have in your mind. Even family, parents, brothers and sisters cannot claim they know us well enough to tell us what we can or cannot do. As a parent myself, I realize that each one of my children has gifts, talents, and abilities that I cannot claim to understand and accurately catalogue but all I can do is wait for them to express what is in them, and then create a suitable environment that would encourage its expression. The greatest mistake I believe I can make is to judge them by my own standards. What if what they have in them is far greater than what I can ever imagine? I would then be a stumbling block to their development rather than a stepping stone for their progress.

So believe in yourself and don't give just anybody the privilege of assessing what is in you. Winston Churchill, Bill Gates, Richard Branson, Martin Luther King Jnr, Abraham Lincoln, Mahatma Gandhi has been known to know their minds and have proceeded accordingly. Every great achiever of every age are only great achievers we remember today because they went against the grain and overcame the assessment and limitations people tried to placed on them.

I must clarify one aspect here before I end this chapter; I spoke about the place and the work of a mentor. The mentor is a person who sees you for who you will become unlike others who see you through their limitations. The mentor is the only one that should be given the allowance to help you factor the pros and cons of any idea that you are thinking on. The mentor is intrinsic to the success you desire. When first things are first then the naysayers will not have any effect on your judgments and implementations.

If God doesn't put any unrealistic limitation on you, my question is -why let man?

So Ladies and Gentlemen, 'Go for it!'

I beseech you to keep moving forward armed with the resolve that you can change your world.

Chapter 7

Projx International

"Motivation is what gets you started.
Habit is what keeps you going".
- Jim Rohn-

ProjX was born out of a conversation two brothers had in their bedroom one Saturday afternoon in 2002. The conversation went something like this – the older brother speaking, "Isn't it a shame that our community is weak on every department; in business we are behind, our country is classed as Third World, the Black race seems to be struggling in every department and to make it worse, we are not united. We don't trust each other and can't work together! I wonder why nobody is doing anything about this. Our predicament is treated like a terminal disease that is handled with the classic denial approach, which is what happens when we human beings are confronted with such insurmountable issues." The older brother was standing beside the double bunk they both used to sleep on. The younger slept on top while the older slept on the bottom bunk. The older sibling had already left the nest and has just come for a short visit.

As he stood there with an air of expectation on the younger brother's response, he didn't expect the younger brother to respond with, "Well, stop talking about all these problems, you go and do something about it, and leave me alone!" The older brother was shocked because he's mild mannered younger brother wasn't prone to such sharp outbursts!

The older brother happened to be me!

I know an outburst when I see one, and not only did it jolt me to take note, I could feel the blood rising in me, not the blood of anger but of determination. The determination that meant that I resolved to hold my tongue behind my teeth and do something about it! I promised myself that the next time my brother was going to hear me speak about these issues; it will be through my actions.

Actions they say speak louder than words!

From that day it took me about 9 months to finally take action, but the thought was never far from my mind. At that time I was working at Tate & Lyle depot and headquarters in Silver town where I worked as a bulk shift clerk. The job paid well, at least better than any job I had before then. But I hated the job. I was in charge of tanker sugar deliveries which comprised of facilitating the smooth operation of tank numbers, driver names, and scheduled destinations.

If a tanker is late, the customer calls me and shouts at me, if a driver's tank was not loaded, he shouts at me, if there was a queue of tankers on the loading bay, the Manager shouts at the supervisor who in turn shouts at me.

I was there for 3yrs I believe, giving the job everything I had, and I never got a thank you, instead the general consensus was the cliché – "you're getting paid to take this crap aren't ya?", and as if that was not deplorable enough on a daily basis the proverbial "Just get on with it", was the sentiment of every poor soul there. Sometimes it felt like I was in a scene of an old western movie. It felt like the drivers would walk in chewing tobacco, let fly a jet of spit that just misses me by an inch then proceed to bark orders at me, while dusting of their hats that always set off a spray of dust, which will finally settle as a film on me and every other thing in the vicinity. I would give them their paper-work (dust and all) like a bar tender that wanted no trouble, ready to dive for cover in case anyone got too excited.

By this time I had had about 10 years of reading motivational books. So I knew I deserved better, which made going in to work another day harder and harder. Everyday had a 3 shift pattern, 6am – 2pm, 2pm – 10pm and then 10pm – 6am. The office never closed and I mean never! There were always three people that manned the bulk shift clerk desk and computers, if someone had to go on holiday, the 2 remaining would cover by doing 12hr shifts instead of 8hrs.

LEAVING MY J.O.B...

I've got to leave this job, I kept telling myself. I had already handed in my resignation twice before. It was tough, like I said the job paid well but it was a hard one. Two colleagues had already had nervous break downs on account of the job - I was sure I was the third if I didn't get out. I was wound up tight; anything could trip me off now. I was like a primed grenade, a cocked magnum saying "do you feel lucky? Well do ya?" I was like a volcano ready to erupt when I finally read "Robert Kiyosaki's The Cash flow quadrant". Talk about an appropriate ice cap!

Half way through the book, I knew I was going to hand in my resignation the third time and this time was the final one and it was for real. I was ready to take the plunge, leave the job, and return to Nigeria to birth ProjX International.

THE RUSSIAN ROULETTE OF LIFE

While I was back in Nigeria in my secondary school days, I went to Federal Government College Maiduguri in the northern part of Nigeria after a brief stint at Eletu-Odibo High School, in the province of Abule Oja.

While at Eletu-Odibo High School I was always one of the top three best students in my class, but when I got to F.G.C Maiduguri I was quickly given a rude and shocking reality check. When exam results came and to my astonishment I wasn't in the top three,

I was convinced someone had made a mistake, I wasn't even in the top 10, not in the top 20, it was the ultimate surreal experience when my name was called at the 32nd position, I knew this wasn't going to be an easy ride, as the multitude ahead of me weren't playing!

Toyin Lawani on the other hand was always bouncing around in the top 10. Academically, I knew Toyin was better than I. Only fate had it that I was born in London and he wasn't, so by 2002 when I heard he was languishing in Nigeria, I knew if he had the chance I had, he would have done better than I, at least he would of fared better than where he was. So I had Toyin in mind when I went to start ProjX international in Nigeria. I knew if Toyin and other friends I had over there had the new information I had gleaned from the books I had read and the people I had met they could change their world even in a harsh environment like Nigeria.

I arrived in Nigeria August 8th 2002 with a suitcase full of books and a dream of transforming lives. I had resigned from Tate & Lyle a couple of months earlier. I remember the day I walked in to my manager's office armed with my resignation letter. He looked up, I gave him the letter, and he took a glance at it, looked up and said "what is it this time? Who has upset you now?" obviously he was referring to my previous attempts to resign.

I remember smiling and assuring him I wasn't upset with anyone, it was just time to go. I remember him asking me this question, "Didn't you say you have two kids and your wife is expecting a third?" I nodded yes and thought isn't that just true of the "system", they pay you enough to feel comfortable, you build a life around your salary; wife, kids and a mortgage, the three most expensive things that happen to all human beings, once that's all clicked in, they know they've got you where they want you, you are locked in for life matey!… that is until the day of retirement when they will give you a gold watch (If you are lucky), to further watch your life go by. I just knew I would fight with all I had not to end up going the direction the "system" pointed.

As soon as I got to Nigeria I started working on my friends. In the end, only Toyin took the ProjX idea seriously and within my 3 months limited stay, we had achieved the goal of running weekly ProjX meetings (after a brief training period with Toyin). ProjX international: an environment where all people grow to become successful entrepreneurs had been born and was now going through its infantile stage.

I remember when it was time to return to the UK, leadership of ProjX Nigeria was handed to Toyin Lawani, and before boarding the plane, Toyin shook my hands and said, "Akin, this few weeks working on this project has been the best time of my entire life" I shook his hands hugged him not knowing that was the last time I would ever see Toyin this side of eternity.

Sadly, Toyin died 28th May 2006 due to a surgery complication while being treated for an ulcer. I pray that his soul rests in perfect peace. This is the Russian roulette of life!

PROJX INTERNATIONAL continued...

When I got back to the UK, my intention wasn't to have ProjX in the UK. I was convinced that people in the UK were too highly strung, and relatively too comfortable to engage a message like ProjX. I admit today that I was so wrong. While ProjX Nigeria continued with Toyin at the helm while he was still alive, I kept in touch via email and phone to hear the latest developments in ProjX Nigeria. Toyin would record the meetings and would send me the tapes. I quickly became astounded at the quick growth they were having. Most especially the rate at which Toyin's personal development was growing. I remember thinking to myself "If I don't have ProjX UK started and have an environment where I can keep myself sharp as Toyin had in Nigeria. I thought to myself that when I go back in a couple of years and discover those guys had progressed so far ahead of me, then people must wonder how I, the founder was now having to play catch up.

I decided I would start ProjX UK, if only to keep myself sharp and on the cutting edge. I remember the first meeting I called. Nobody showed! I had spent the last week inviting people and still nobody showed. Here I was in an empty room, the board and easel was set, the markers were primed. The chairs were arranged in a meeting fashion, even though it was my mother's living room. I was dressed in my best suit and nobody showed? I was faced with only two last choices; it's either I pack everything up and cancel the meeting or have a meeting with me, myself and I, not forgetting the Holy Trinity that had laid this vision on my heart.

I decided to have the meeting even if I was the only one there physically. I prayed and called myself to attention, announced to myself that the meeting was starting, said hello to myself and proceeded to talk to an empty room; why ProjX and why now? About 30 minutes into my meeting of one, I heard the door to the sitting room open slowly with a soft squeal; my younger sister's head poked in cautiously, seeing me and surveying the empty sitting room. "What are you doing?" she asked. "Having a meeting" I replied, she looked around the room again to make sure she hadn't missed anything, "Meeting with whom?" she asked, "Well I invited people to this meeting but nobody showed" I said.

In explanation I offered, "So I decided to have the meeting regardless!" I was appreciative of having a conversation with somebody even if it was a barrage of curious questions. My sister said, "Well I'll see you later", as she left the room. I must admit I had half hoped she would stay but with my determination still intact I proceeded to have an hour of me speaking to an empty room.

That experience convinced me that I was totally committed to the vision with or without support.

Amazingly that was my first and last meeting of one, because from the next meeting to my writing this book, ProjX has developed a very healthy following and today even if I don't show up, people will; which proves once again that there is no stopping an idea whose time has come.

WHY CALL IT PROJX?

ProjX I admit is an unusual name but one with a meaning. ProjX is an entity, a Spirit; an empowering spirit, a cooperative spirit, an inspirational and motivational spirit, and a 'can do' spirit.

I didn't want to call it 'business this' or 'business that' with its many connotations. While growing up in Nigeria I was exposed to the common assumption that when people employed the word 'business' they usually demonstrated what they meant by tapping the side of their nose and winking at you. Apart from that the word 'business' kind of has this never ending connotation, the picture I get is of something that goes on and on and on, with no end in sight.

A project on the other hand, has the implication of something starting with an end date in mind; at which one can assess; was one successful or not. ProjX as an idea has always been one that seeks to empower others, and is designed to accommodate ideas other people have for the sole purposes of helping them achieve their goal. Now since one cannot predict what ideas people are carrying, how can one reflect that in the name? That is where the 'X' Factor comes in. Now instead of calling it Project X, I noticed that the 'ect' part of the word Project could be replaced by 'X' and still sound like project when pronounced together. The name ProjX was born, and that is why the X at the end of the name is always a capital 'X'.

ProjX international is an organization that provides an environment where other companies can thrive in a community of other companies. Now each company has its vision, mission and objectives; The 'X' in ProjX is there to reflect one, all and any company that joins the ProjX family of companies. This is subject to the amicability of the mission statement and criteria.

Just thought you might want to know.

Our Motto:

"An environment where people grow to become successful entrepreneurs."

REMEMBER: YOU CANNOT DRIFT UP THE MOUNTAIN

Most people I observe live their lives in a fashion that telegraph their overall philosophy to life; they would do only enough and the least they can get away with, and they expect that to be enough to get them to the top. They would do only what they are told and put all their hopes on the government, their boss, their company, their parents, the popular trends and what everyone else believes in, and they think that is enough to take them to their desired destination.

90% of the world's wealth is in the hands of 1% of the world's population and 5% of the remaining wealth is in the control of 4% of the population, while the remaining 5% of the world's wealth is shared among 95% of the worlds population. The overwhelming reason why 95% of the world's population shares only 5% of the world's wealth is simply because they never do their own research, they rely on the news and popular belief systems to inform them. They feel safe only when they are part of the herd. On the other hand the rich and super rich, invest all their time in doing their own research, seeking out hidden information and trends to form their own strategy. They never follow trends, they set the trends that others are forced to follow.

To change our world, we must all be avid students of life, and the forces that act upon it, otherwise the only other option is to be tossed to and fro, by every and any wind of doctrine, trend, circumstances and disaster. Some people want to change their world yet they would not seek out information, they will not read, they will not focus and discipline themselves to pay the price it takes to really change their world. **THESE SORTS OF PEOPLE DELUDE THEMSELVES! THEY WILL ALWAYS BE STUCK IN A RUT UNTIL THEY DECIDE TO PAY THE PRICE FOR THE KIND OF LIFE THEY DESIRE.**

What the rich know and take very seriously, that the poor and middle classes are ignoring at their peril:

THE "GET A DEGREE" MANTRA:

Go to school, get a degree, then get a good job and you will be successful; this kind of plan is now unfortunately a recipe for disaster.

I am not against getting a degree; by all means get all the degrees your heart desires

What I am against is this notion that the degree in itself is enough for a successful life.

No! In today's world a degree is no longer a barometer for success, and I agree for most it's far better to go for and have a degree, but it is no longer the meal ticket it used to be in the past.

The education required for true success is now found beyond the walls of academia.

JOB FOR LIFE:

There used to be a term "Job for life" that is now no longer valid. The rich don't rely on jobs for their lifestyle. The poor and middle class unfortunately do.

IT'S THE GOVERNMENTS JOB TO TAKE CARE OF US:

The expectation that governments will take care of us is altogether a naïve expectation. Governments are not parents or guardians, Governmental structures are instruments created by the people for the people. We are the Government; which means Governments cannot take care of people; people will ultimately have to take care of themselves, especially with regards to individual successes and futures.

THE GOVERNMENT WILL TELL ME WHAT TO BELIEVE:

Another naïve belief! The Government and media are controlled by special interests and do not exist to inform the masses accurately, in fact they are now there to misinform. A case in point is - The Iraq War and weapons of mass destruction.

JUST WORK HARD, THINGS WILL WORK IF ONLY YOU WORKED HARD!

We all know people, I believe images of people you know are coming to your mind right now; people who are working hard, working so hard and are still working hard and getting nowhere. No, just hard work is never enough; you've got to work smart.

The man selling burgers at the street corner and Mc Donald's are both selling burgers.

The difference one is working hard and the other is working smart.

MONEY IN THE BANK WILL PROTECT ME FROM ANY ECONOMIC CRISIS:

Not necessarily, your money has forces like inflation and deflation working on it constantly, the belief that paper money is money is another erroneous belief that sets people up for disaster! Money follows value, in the 1930s Germany experienced Hyper-inflation; people carried paper money in wheel barrows to buy a loaf of bread.

Create value and build networks as those are the true levers of wealth.

DEBT IS GOOD! OR DEBT IS BAD!

The rich know it's not the debt that is good or bad, but the strategy the investor employs that is good or bad. There is no good or bad investment, only good or bad investors.

The list goes on and on…

I will not attempt to cover everything on this subject in this book, my intention here is to help you identify a few and invite you to do a little bit of research. Remember success is a journey, not a destination! So start your own journey now.

ProjX international provides an environment that engenders this much needed focus and discipline required to really change one's world and remain in charge. It provides a constant place to associate with people serious about effecting this change. It provides a platform to articulate one's thoughts and beliefs by encouraging all participants to speak publicly, this creates an extremely rich pool of information and intellectual capital.

ANYONE CAN START THEIR OWN

Anyone with a heart for people and a desire to empower people can start an outfit like ProjX international and enjoy the amazing benefits that come with it. If you want to put together weekly meetings that will start empowering your immediate network, I will say go for it, it is desperately needed. Our community is so uninformed that it is beyond the alarming. I encourage any move towards the ultimate reality of the purpose all persons long for.

The reward for serving your network in this fashion is well worth it. Try it and see, but make sure you do it with a pure motive, if you desire to see the right result. Intent is everything.

Many people have been touched by ProjX international

We have had people join us years ago that are unrecognizable by people that knew them before the ProjX influence. Lives have changed, families transformed, life-time relationship have been forged and continue to be strengthened.

Influencing ideas have been and continue to be born and nurtured to the point where they are now flourishing. Problems are being solved; the network is getting stronger by helping people become stronger.

PAGES FROM SOME BALCONY PEOPLE

To this end, I introduce a fraction of the men and women who have been touched by ProjX International. Here they share in their own words what it means to be part of the dream manifesting phenomenon that is ProjX International.

Listen to their well chosen words of before and after with the added element of progress. You will identify with them and I believe you will desire to achieve what they have accomplished so far. Could it be that you the reader will have the opportunity to add his/her story in a publication like the one you are holding in your hand right now? Lastly, I encourage you to pursue excellence with a pure intent to succeed and carry others with you. Come join the balcony people.

Mr. Phil on…Zari:

One should never underestimate the power of walking up to a "stranger" and saying 'hello'. I was at a Men's conference and while time was allowed for a short break I spotted this gentleman and thought, "well, go say hello". Then the battle started, shall I? Or Shall I not? Oh I can't be bothered... on and on the battle went. Thankfully I bothered; I walked up to this "stranger" with a smile and said "hello, my name is Philip".

Little did I know that this "stranger" was really a great friend and brother, and a kindred spirit! I remember asking him what he did, and he told me he was a poet and writer, at which point I told him I was writing my first book, and that maybe he would care to read it and tell me what he thought. Nothing happened for the next 2 months. I invited him to our Tuesday meeting and he came, yet still nothing happened until one day he told me he had started editing the book you now hold in your hand; the rest as they say is history. A chance hello introduced me to the last jigsaw in the puzzle of getting this book in your hand. I thank God I didn't miss saying that destiny fulfilling "hello", and I thank Zari for his faithfulness and commitment to doing his bit in making this dream come true.

In Zari's own words;

The men's meeting was in session. The keynote speaker was motivating and enthralling as he orated his point with the precision of a surgeon. The audience of men sat and sensed destiny laced with the ability to make it happen. This conference was set to be a first of many. I was part of the planning team and this exposed me to the highs and lows of organizing something of this magnitude. There at this conference I noticed a tall gentleman who wore the broadest smile I had ever seen a black man wear. We all smile sheepishly at best but this fellow's beaming dentition lit up the room like floodlights on a dark night. My attention was caught as he approached me, still beaming and speaking with his signature booming voice that arrests a room.

We exchanged details and shared banter as the conference continued in essence. The fellow of which

I speak is Mr. Phil. He shared his influencing idea regarding ProjX with such astuteness I was compelled to check him out. He invited me to one his meetings where he waxed lyrical about the backbone and intent of ProjX. I sat there drinking in the possibilities of a new way of thinking and implementing the outcome.

Mr. Phil proceeded to invite me to address the room full of people as he did the others in the room. This was a first for me in such a setting. I am a public speaker so I delivered what my heart felt and saw, which was revealing. ProjX International is new to me and me to it yet I can see the difference clearly in the vision of one man who was not afraid to move forward regardless of obstacles. I am moved when I see a man like Mr. Phil who believes in his gut that the difficult is not impossible. Recently, as we spoke one evening he let the cat out of the bag that he had written this book. In the course of our discussion I divulged that I was a writer, poet, and sometime editor amongst other talents I hone daily. Mr. Phil promptly emailed me the book and trusted me to do what I do best.

At the time of writing this page, Mr. Phil asked me to tag along to a specialist satellite TV and radio station in South London for a screen test. The idea was to get presenters to front a new format of programming. We couldn't grasp the providence that welcomed us into that studio. Would you believe we presented a live radio slot for 30 minutes and get this, we both co-hosted a live TV show that was broadcast throughout Africa. What are the odds that this could occur without a person of tenacity like Mr. Phil? ProjX International is headed for success with a company of people who accept themselves for who they are; Winners. I now lend my gifts to ProjX International not because it is another vehicle for selfish gain but for the furtherance of others and the manifesting of the best that the present and the future hold.

ProjX International is like no other by the sheer fact that it exists because the parts are as important as the whole. Mr. Phil is an individual who is a visionary with a twist. He shares and explains the whole picture of personal development, motivation and radical business information. Don't take my word for it, I dare you to come and see and hear the phenomenon at work. Ask yourself these questions; who do I believe I am purposed to be? Am I happy with my life? What can I do to change it?

If you are like me and you know that the dream you dream is closer than you imagine, go ahead and take a leap of faith. I promise you this, slowly but surely you will not recognize yourself, as change will have given you the treasures to bloom. You can change your world. One thought at a time.

zari alexxanderr-caine, Poet, Writer,
Editor, Life-Style Facilitator and Speaker

Mr. Phil on…Akinleye:

Picture this; we are in the trenches, in the middle of a terrible war! Bullets are whizzing around, mortars are pounding, and men lose their heads to bullets just for raising their heads an inch. Which man would you want beside you in those trenches? I can say emphatically that I will choose Akinleye any day to be in the trenches with me, why? Let me answer that: There are those that talk the talk, but unlike them Akinleye walks the walk. Akinleye has earned my respect and the respect of many others. I have seen this gentleman live the principles outlined in this book for many years and he continues to change his world! I have seen him pay the price for success, while others scramble around looking for shortcuts. We are all works in progress, like a statue in the hand of a sculptor; we must all chisel away at ourselves, getting rid of all the unwanted debris in our lives. With this in mind, a man must then be fashioned by the tools he uses on himself. Akinleye Akintunde is chiseling away frantically and I am convinced we are beholding a masterpiece.

In Akinleye's own words;

We sometimes get so transfixed on our destination rather than enjoying the journey. I tell new members of Projx International after their first meeting that their journey has just begun. I am not sure if any one of them really understand me but off they go until they reach the first check point. What are check points?

These are simple tasks and instructions that are given to them, that when completed moves them to the next level of development.

My journey started over 15 years ago now when my curiosity got the better of me. this happened when my brother, Philip had met a successful gentleman that arranged to explain Philip's new found excitement to our father. I sneaked in to listen to the presentation. All I remembered about the evening was that here was somebody more successful than us all at that time, and he was willing to help us. Little did I know, at the time that it went beyond the man in our midst. Somebody once said that "you will be the same in 5 years time except for two things. The people you meet and the books you read". I will modify it to say that you will be the same in 5 years except for the people you meet. This is because the people you meet will recommend the books you should read.

I started off very excited only to be brought back to reality by the toughest and most challenging of people around me (my family and friends). Once these are conquered, the rest of the population I was told are a lot easier.

My first failings only identified that I lacked the required skills. It taught me that failure is never final if you don't quit. Failures are stepping stones to success.

As your skill level increases you will discover that your success ratio also improves. It's just that simple, no magic formula. I went from a shy teenager to becoming very skilled in meeting new people whilst turning cold contacts into friends and then they became family.

I quickly learnt to enjoy my development journey and learnt not to be deterred by the initial discouraging results. My motto became - I will until I succeed. I realized that I was always learning from each failure and then began to appreciate that I was getting better. I kept improving to the point that Mr. Phil now calls me a master.

We must focus on getting everything out of each moment, as Jim Rohn would say, "Wherever you are, be there!" That statement is both simple and powerful. Each moment that constitutes "the present" is to be savoured. Enjoy the journey as you go forth and remain successful. Remember: success is not a destination, it's a journey. So enjoy it!

Akinleye Akintunde, Investment Banker and the Co-founder of ProjX International

---

Mr. Phil on… Anaya:

Anaya is somebody that deserves to be noted in a book titled 'You Can Change Your World'. Here was a young lady trudging along in life until life gave her a challenge, 'be average or be special!' Anaya chose to be special, and then she chose to pay the price for being special and has never looked back.

I call her a woman among men. At ProjX we have had a lot of women join our meetings and workshops, but no other woman has endorsed, embraced and represented what we stand for like Anaya has. Anaya has proven herself many times over as someone who will stand for what she believes in. When the battle of life rages, these are the kind of people I want around me. Anaya is the type you know will not leave her station for the enemy to invade.

Thanks for being you Anaya; the world sure needs many more like you.

In Anaya's own words:

Hmm... what can I say? I have come a long, long, long way. I am blessed and fortunate to be at the right place at the right time. Born into an Islamic and well known established family in Sierra Leone, I have always had the skill of selling and making profit but it was always only displayed innocently. I was not really conscious of my gift until now that I look back, and realize I have always been entrepreneurial.

Talking about being in the right place at the right time, just after I left Islam to follow Christ, I met Akinleye in a young Christian's class, where his introduction to me was made by a tremendous beaming smile. I was taken aback by this young gentleman looking straight at me and beaming from ear to ear. This wasn't a common situation, so my curiosity was aroused enough that I was the first to say "Hello brother" little did I know my life was just about to change again irrevocably.

Akinleye invited me to a business function and later introduced me to his brother who is the author of this book and this entirely new world of business empowerment opened up before me. Thanks to you Akinleye, because you where the one the Lord used to open the door that I stepped through. I discovered ProjX International, a unique environment where I could attend meetings at no cost, and have access to self development material and teachings that so impacted my life that my life literally changed.

Just being around the right people and the right environment such as ProjX International has changed my world. I feel so privileged and blessed to have experienced the journey I have with an amazing bunch of like-minded people. In life I have found what you need are good friends and family. If I am truthful sometimes friends are there much more than family are.

ProjX International is true to its motto: "An environment where people grow to be successful entrepreneurs" What I learnt from ProjX has made me become far more confident in dealing with people and dealing with huge life challenges. I owe my popularity amongst friends and family to all the things I learnt from ProjX. ProjX has been a massive force behind me.

Self development is something that is crucial in today's world. It is what gave me a fighting chance against the old programming I had. It helped me break my old thinking pattern, which was selfish, self centered, self seeking, and generally disempowering. I look back now and wonder where I will be today if I wasn't exposed to what I have been exposed to through ProjX. It frightens me to even imagine the alternative life I would have now if I didn't invest in my self-development.

The tips below are the tools I have personally used to change my world. It is not an overnight thing; I have had to apply these tools to my life diligently. I find in life all you need to change is yourself, because when you change your world changes.

Anaya's tips on changing your world:

1. Be open to change.
2. Be honest with yourself.
3. Be willing to grow.
4. Don't quit.
5. Have integrity.
6. Always have the right 'Motive'.
7. Look out for the need in others and help fill it.
8. Always have the right attitude as it will always take you places.
9. Give, give yourself, give of yourself and give genuinely.
10. Lead; Leadership is everything, but remember be a leader not a boss.

Anaya Hajah Yabome Kamara,
Business woman

Mr. Phil on... Johnson:

Mr. Johnson Olukotun has been a breath of fresh air when it comes to the right kind of attitude every gentleman or woman should have towards being teachable. He is willing to learn, embracing change, and never believing that one knows it all. He is a very experienced and powerful man in every respect. When he met us, he took his time to listen, was open and with inquisitiveness almost as that of an innocent child, this man who was already far more experienced than most in our network, showed the wisdom of the wise, by not dismissing the new paradigm he saw in ProjX, but rather persevered until he caught the spirit of ProjX.

That I noted was the mark of a great man, and as we got to know Johnson Olukotun I personally saw for sure, this was a great man. Today Johnson is a pillar in the ProjX network, a soldier in every sense of the word especially for Christ.

In Johnson's own words;

Could you believe that a simple hand shake could be a turnaround experience for a seasoned veteran? Here is a man that has served in the Nigerian Navy for ten good years. Having travelled the world and experienced what very few can ever experience in one lifetime; I met a young friendly gentleman with the warmest smile you have ever seen, this was out of place especially in this age where you hardly bother to keep eye contact, talk less of smiling. My encounter on that great evening at Tesco in Romford marked the beginning of a life changing experience even for a veteran like me.

That five to ten minute encounter with a gentleman called Akinleye, marked the beginning of my entrepreneurial journey. I was invited to a ProjX meeting where I met some enterprising young men and women full of life.

I couldn't spend much time with them that night as I was on night shift as a care worker. Just a few minutes of interaction with these young people made me decide I mustn't leave without getting a few contact details. That was my first experience of ProjX.

The next meeting I could attend was about 3 months later, where I remember vividly Philip saying "You will never be rich unless you work for yourself". When I heard that it blew my mind, because at that point in my life, I was struggling with a business idea that could make or break me. I was afraid of taking the plunge into the unknown, and to make matters even more complicated I had just recently relocated to the UK after sojourning in Germany for 13 years.

After the meeting I arranged a one on one meeting with Philip, Adebola Mogaji and another member of ProjX, where the concept "Bump Centre International" was born. Bump Centre International is today known as the only centre in the whole world that uses herbal therapies with unquestionable results, for razor bumps, keloids, acne and various other skin conditions that conventional medicine is still to find lasting solutions for. After this meeting I decided to meet Philip one on one on a regular basis because I saw the empowerment I was getting, and the speed at which my dreams were becoming a reality. ProjX international now became an environment where I saw steady growth in myself and my business. ProjX is the first and only place I have ever seen, where more than thirty people would gladly help promote your product and service vigorously at no charge. They have proven genuinely that it is only to empower you. It is also at ProjX I met professional people like Michael Frempong –Taylor, a business consultant who has used his wealth of experience in consultancy to help create a system for the Bumps Centre.

I met people like Kameel, a financial service guru who has helped negotiate competitive professional indemnity liability insurance, which has been a burden since the inception of the Bumps Centre. He has also helped to set up a franchise agreement. I also met Byo Moby, a pharmacologist who has help propel the Bumps Centre to a level where we are now able to combine forces with medical practitioners and professionals who are helping in carrying out evidence based research on the Bump Centre therapy for the treatment of Bumps and Keloid.

My experience at ProjX has indeed changed my mind set about my entrepreneurial journey. It has taught me to think first of how to be a blessing to others before thinking of what I am going to get. To get the best from an environment like ProjX, people have to come with a mind of how to give to others because only then would they find themselves qualified for the kind of blessing I have received from this amazing group.

Johnson Olukotun, Keloid Skin Specialist

While we cannot in one book feature everyone that have been part of the ProjX journey, we however offer you a few more:

Mary Daniels

Mary is one of those special ladies that come along very seldom in business life. She's a lady with tremendous business skills and personality, Mary's contribution to the ProjX Network has been exemplary. Mary is now based in Malaysia after a few years of building businesses and relationships in the UK. Experienced in retail outlets, Mary once facilitated in growing a Marks & Spencer type establishment to over 20 shops overseeing thousands of employed staff. Mary's skill with people has left a legacy within the network, expressed in the business relationships that continue to blossom internationally between our UK and Malaysian contacts. If there is any credit to be given for all the positive things happening now between our UK and Malaysian contacts the credit is all Mary's.

Ben Raj Raju and Uma Sundram

These Directors of Worldfone communications are examples of Mary's positive success stories within our network. As we hold ProjX meetings every Tuesday night, Mary invited Benjamin to our meeting apparently to meet some new business contacts who could be instrumental in helping to expand his telecommunication business.

Benjamin, armed with an open mind came to check out our meeting and must have liked what he saw because he has since worked with us successfully on several projects and if the plans we have for the future is anything to go by, there are many more successful joint exploits to look forward to.

Uma Sundram the other part of the dynamic duo of Directors in Worldfone, has been a pleasure to work with. Endowed with a "can do" attitude, Uma gets on with the challenge of building and maintaining new business ideas and structures with ease. Happy to think outside the box to solve business problems, she is tireless in her quest of getting things done. I am yet to see any challenge that can stand this lady's temerity. Uma has become another asset to the ProjX network as a whole.

Edward Adeleye

A member of ProjX from its onset, Edward has always been one that has seen the potential of a Network like ours and has been proclaiming the future with the vigour of a prophet within our midst.

A gentle giant with a big heart, Edward embraced the value of working together with ease while others were either skeptical or cynical. Having being burnt several times in business deals, he is someone with enough experiences in the past to doubt the prospects of working together. Not Edward, on the contrary Edward bounded with great strides in working with people unreserved and with admirable optimism.

Byo Moby

Byo is one of the rare individuals whose example of looking out for the progress and success of others should be emulated by all. He is a family man, a man of faith, a business man, Networker, Artist, Business Coach, Mentor, and a very close friend. Byo's energy, enthusiasm, creativity, and drive is always spent in pursuit of other people's benefit. In a community like ours I am sure we will all agree that this kind of quality in a man is very rare.

A man whose network spans the globe, Byo has been a fierce supporter of ProjX International and Mr. Phil. He often does this by promoting our values, filming our events, helping us strategize, plan and execute our desire to empower our community. A man with great resources and skill set, Byo continues to share, teach, equip, and release the young, middle aged and old every chance he gets.

Akin George

Akin George heard about ProjX from a business colleague and did what very few people do, he walked into one of our meeting sessions, introduced himself with words along this line "Mrs so and so recommended I come and see what is going on here, and to also see how we can be of mutual benefit". That was almost 3years ago, Akin George since then has proven himself a valuable ProjX member. He is someone who espouses the value of seeking information, assimilating and elevating ones awareness in a quest for continuous growth.

The Akin George of 3yrs ago is definitely not the Akin George of today. He has grown and continues to grow by demanding of himself a standard of excellence that is uncommon in our environment. We at ProjX value such dedication to growth above most other qualities, we believe growth to be an ongoing process, one which almost guarantees the equipping and character required for true success.

Niyi Soremekun

A quiet and thinking man, Niyi came into the ProjX environment; a paradigm shifting environment, a paradigm questioning environment; and it's never easy to be open minded enough to have our belief systems challenged, stripped and now after careful deliberation accept and adopt a paradigm. Very few people have the mental fortitude to embrace a new paradigm; Niyi has proven himself to belong to this class of "very few".

Niyi's type of attitude to embracing new concepts, new outlooks, new and better ways of doing things, is one of the qualities that I respect the most in people. I expect great things from this quiet but powerful gentleman.

Simon Wilcox:

Simon got to know about ProjX through sheer persistence, a network like ours has many business expressions and applications; Simon was in the process of expanding a business project of his when he was encouraged to call us. After many times and months of trying to reach us, we finally met and have since embarked on building and activating several networks.

A natural networker, Simon is a tireless self developer, someone sold out to the concept of working on himself more than anybody else; this makes for the kind of leadership we value in ProjX. The kind of leadership the world needs right now. We live in times of great change and it is anticipated that these changes will happen quicker and more people will need to take responsibility for their own welfare. The government will not be able to help as it did in the past, which means people will have to be far more enterprising than they have been in the past, hence a special kind of leadership is required, one that says "do as I do, not do as I say". Simon is such an individual that fosters this philosophy.

Pastor Gabriel. A. Ilori

Our paths crossed with Pastor Ilori, at Odua TV station, courtesy of Byo Moby's invitation. From the start we were impressed with Pastor Ilori's openness and willingness to learn whilst he exuded a rare kind of genuine humility. A very popular radio ministry personality in his own right, one supposes he could be forgiven if he succumbed to the temptation of impressing upon us his pedigree and achievements; you know the one that barks "don't you know who I am?" type expression.

Pastor Ilori proved to be everything but that as we got to know him better as he earned our respect the right way through a teachable and servant's heart.

As a network, we are proud to be working with Pastor Ilori on several projects. Ours is a network that grows by helping others grow. Pastor Ilori recognized that the philosophy of growing by helping other's grow is the height of greatness, expressed by Jesus Christ when he said "the greatest amongst you shall be the servant of all!" He is a pastor who believes in empowering his radio listeners and local congregation to achieve their God given potential. Our money is on Pastor Ilori setting an example for other leaders that it is profitable to put the needs of the people first and above their needs. We look forward to God doing great things with this servant of the Most High God.

Notes

Every page in this book is littered with quotes, which I have gleaned from the literature that I have read on the various subjects I share in this volume. Some of them were discovered on the World Wide Web.

A few are mine because I believe that every man can think, hence, they can share their experiences in a quote. You do not have to be well known to be able to write a quote. You can live with a philosophy that reaches others in so many ways that your words will transcend your existence.

The quotes in this book are well written and the author is accredited with its originality. The books I read are also indicated on the pages that I refer to them. I do this so that I give credit to those who have gone ahead of us and have paid the price. I encourage you to invest in yourself. Try as you may to get the books I have mentioned and you too can reach the realms of success beyond your wildest dreams.

To quote the late great thought leader Jim Rohn, "Each of us needs all of us".

Now that is a quote worthy of much contemplation!

Acknowledgements

I thank God and my Lord and Saviour Jesus Christ for the grace he furnished me to write this book. My brother Dapo Akintunde who was the very first person whose help I enlisted in perusing and editing while I was molding, shaping and articulating what I already felt and saw in my mind's eye. All the people that have in some way, shape or form left a mark on my life, whether you know it or not, I thank you all.

I thank my immediate family; father Mr. Ishola Adesoye Akintunde, my mother Mrs. Esther Tinuola Akintunde, my sister Mrs. Adedayo Alli-Olugbode, Akinleye Akintunde, Michael-Taiwo Akintunde, and Kehinde Akintunde. Ours is a special family and I thank God for blessing me with you all.

Zari Alexxanderr-Caine, this book was in the freezer for over 2yrs, I just couldn't proceed until our chance meeting. Now I know the book was waiting for you, I thank you again for your being 'sold out' to helping other people achieve their God sent purpose. Thank you very much, and may the Lord God bless you and yours real good.

My ProjX family, I thank you for buying into a seemingly crazy idea. All the people on the ProjX mailing list, too numerous to mention all your names here, but if you get emails from ProjX World you know who you are. Thank you so much, the journey has just started, we haven't seen anything yet!

Finally I would like to acknowledge my wife and kids.

Mrs. Adetokunbo Akintunde, Aderiyike Akintunde, Oluwakorede Akintunde, Akintomiwa Akintunde, Akinlekan Akintunde. Yours is the greatest sacrifice, every ProjX expense at the beginning came from the family's coffers, expense in time spent away from you all and money spent in the quest to help others. I am so indebted to you all for your sacrifices that continues even as I type, what I can't repay I pray God will.

Journal pages…

Mr Phil

Journal pages…

And it begins…
Book two is on the way;

Mr Phil's
YOU
Can
Continue to
CHANGE
Your
WORLD

* 9 7 8 1 8 4 4 2 6 9 6 5 5 *

ND - #0181 - 060826 - C0 - 197/132/13 - PB - 9781844269655 - Gloss Lamination